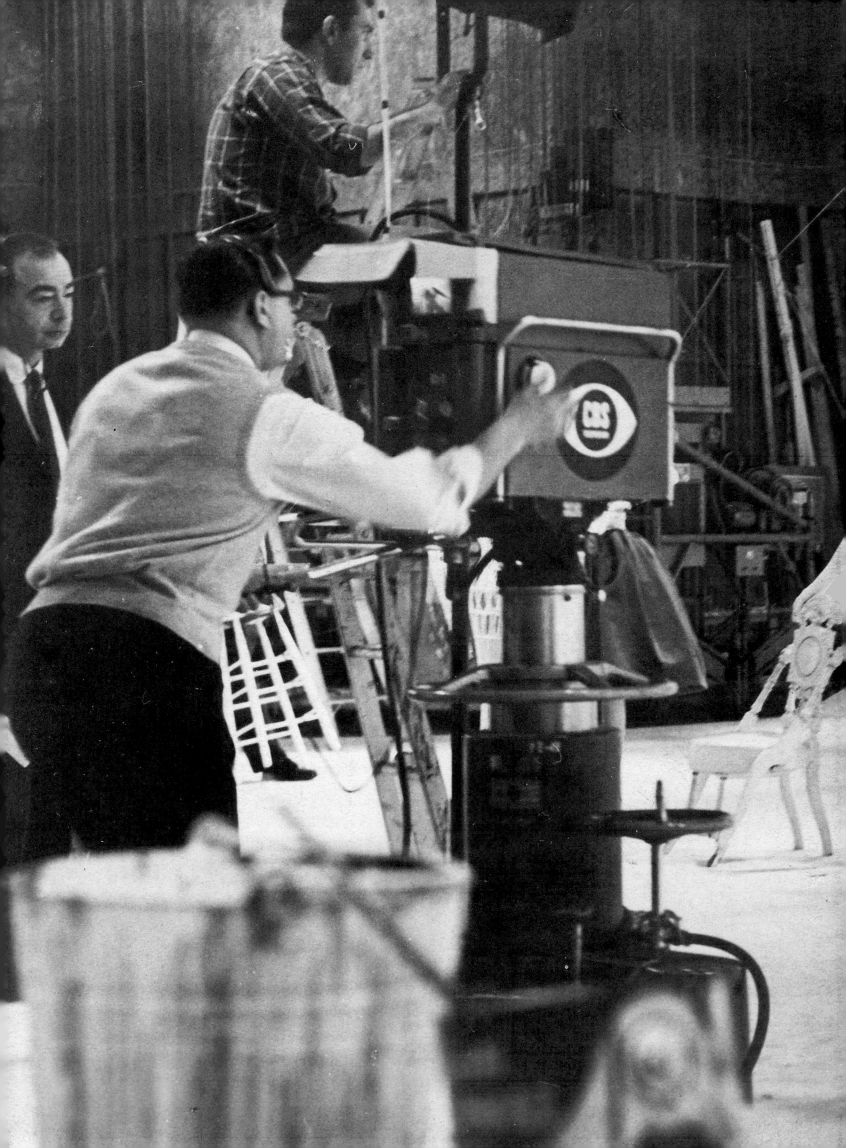

THE GOLDEN AGE OF
TELEVISION

RICK MARSCHALL

SMITHMARK

This edition published in 1995 by SMITHMARK Publishers Inc., 16 East 32nd Street New York, New York 10016

SMITHMARK books are available for bulk purchase for sales promotion and premium use. For details write or telephone the Manager of Special Sales, SMITHMARK Publishers Inc., 16 East 32nd Street, New York, NY 10016. (212) 532-6600.

Produced by Brompton Books Corp., 15 Sherwood Place Greenwich, CT 06830

ISBN 0-8317-3926-6

Printed in China

10 9 8 7 6 5 4 3 2 1

PREVIOUS SPREAD: *Jackie Gleason on the CBS-TV soundstage.*

RIGHT: *Clayton Moore, as the Lone Ranger, and Jay Silverheels (a former national lacrosse champion from Canada) as his faithful Indian companion Tonto. The Lone Ranger was one of the most successful of television's Westerns preceding the 'adult Westerns' of the mid-Golden Age.*

CONTENTS

FOREWORD

Television was an overnight success that was decades in the making. Both scientists and poets had dreamed of a personal medium for communicating images and sound for years before the many technical components were put into place. Massive obstacles to the problems of definition, compatibility and resolution meant that no one person or nation can be credited with the invention of television. Even when the medium became viable, there were problems of manufacturing, affordability and program creation to be resolved. The fickle muse of technology, as well as Depression and war, impeded the progress of television's popularity until 1948.

The period between 1948 and 1960 may be justly described as the Golden Age of television. It was in the post-World War II era that programming exploded to fill the airwaves with exciting shows and the medium's first major stars. By 1960 the original shows, formats and stars had evolved to a point that marks off a new era, and television was experiencing the changes and crises of its second age.

The Golden Age in America was dominated by four networks: ABC, CBS, DuMont and NBC. British television, as overviewed by David Lazell, had both the BBC and independent programming. Nostalgia and reputations can play funny tricks: not all of vintage television was excellent, and some of what is remembered fondly would be better forgotten. What seems like a milestone can sometimes be a millstone. But overall, it was an era of excitement and innovation, and much of early television was both brilliant and unique – pieces of our past that deserve to be recalled. Both the good and the bad are recorded here, the idealism and the moments that fell short of the ideal.

In one short period – the dozen or so years that comprise the Golden Age – America adopted a new obsession that evolved into an irreducible part of our culture and the world's. Television reveals unerringly something about ourselves. What we watch, what we enjoy, what we tune out, even what fails to outrage us, all reflect the society of which we are constituents. In the new age of information technology, many children see more of television than of their fathers, and can recite advertising jingles before their national anthems. Public opinion is formed by news broadcasts, and issues of national and global importance are affected by their presentation on television. The genesis of all this was during the Golden Age.

My students in television history at New York's School of Visual Arts (most of them born after the Golden Age ended) are constantly – and pleasantly – surprised by the wealth and quality of Golden Age television. Whether one remembers or discovers, there is much in the recent past of this magical entertainment medium to appreciate and, it is hoped, to learn from. Stay tuned.

— RICHARD MARSCHALL

RIGHT: One of the enduring memories of Golden Age television, at least to children of the era, is the Mickey Mouse Club. Every day's program was full of production numbers, cartoons, and running serials.

VARIETY
The Spice of Television

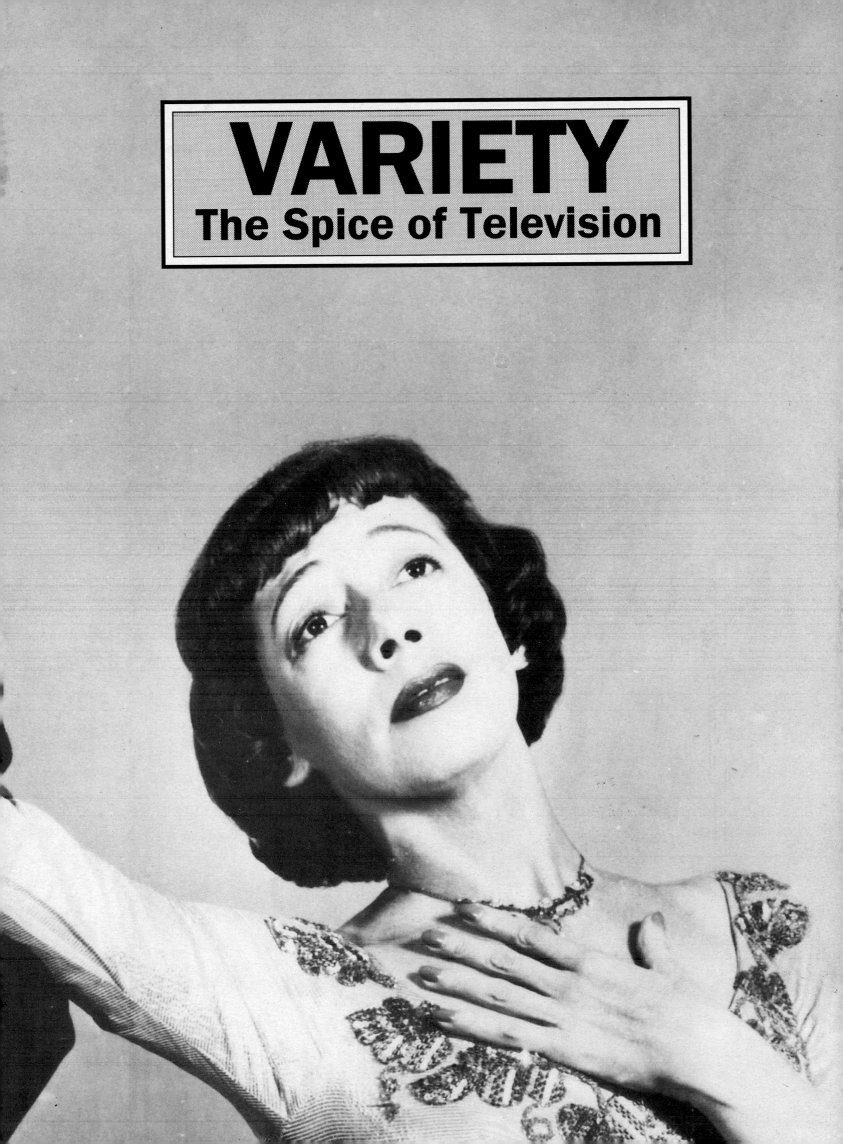

From the very first days of television, when the Golden Age was establishing itself, live drama was its hallmark and the situation comedy can be considered its trademark. But it was the variety show that put television on the map.

For all the executives, technicians, performers, producers and directors who were contributing in a myriad of innovative ways to the exciting new medium, it was a burlesque comedian who blackened his teeth, hit people in their posteriors with bladders, and wore women's dresses, who was virtually knighted as 'Mr Television.' Milton Berle was his name, and he was representative of an army of variety-show hosts – some a bit more dignified – who were responsible for the sales of millions of television sets.

In 1948 Texaco was convinced of television's future, and it transferred its 'Star Theatre' from radio to TV. Its creative staff also intuitively made a shift from a drama-and-variety format to a comedy-variety showcase. Berle was, at the time of these deliberations, the host of the company's radio program in a guest slot, and he was tried as the first host of the television 'Star Theatre.' Then, in a rotating system of on-the-job auditions for the eventual regular show, Berle was followed on succeeding weeks by Henny Youngman, Morey Amsterdam, George Price, Jack Carter, Peter Donald and Harry Richman. Berle then acted as host several more times. Overwhelming audience and critical response convinced Texaco and NBC that his chemistry was right for the show – and for the small screen.

Television receivers were relatively primitive in 1948 – the small screen was *very* small, with flickering images and inconsistent resolution – and Milton Berle's routines were perfect for the huddled masses yearning to see clear. His stage settings were basic, just like a vaudeville stage; the camera angles were straight-on, with few pans or cuts. The costumes were loud, which allowed few viewers to miss any visual item, and the noise level was high too – shouts, screams, sound effects, whoops of laughter – leaving no nuance too slight for sets or viewers to miss. It was a perfect marriage, and somehow even the throwback to vaudeville and burlesque (rather than more recent theatrical refinements) seemed symbolic. Viewers sensed that they were pioneers in an uninhibited field no less than did the performers and producers.

Berle was not the very first in his field. Ted Mack's 'Original Amateur Hour' was a popular fixture on DuMont, beginning early in 1948. It had been a radio success, and can be called a variety program, but without the big-name stars

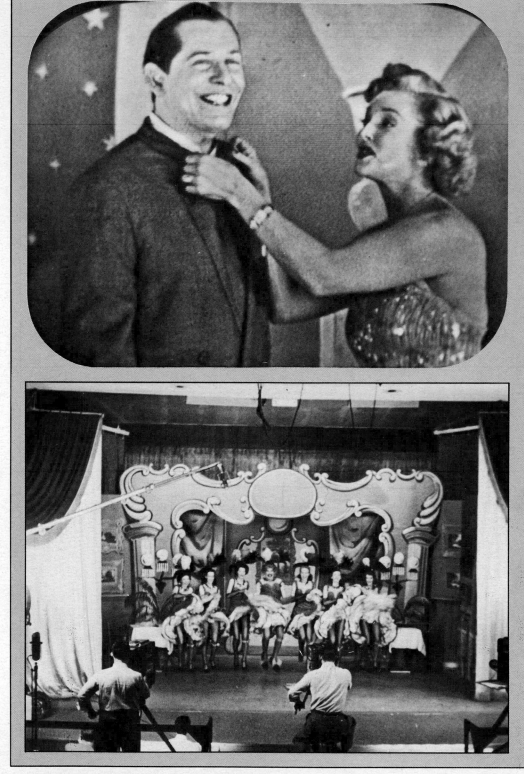

that Berle was to feature. As Major Bowes had done before him, Mack offered a potpourri of hopeful, and mostly awful, talent that nevertheless was popular with viewers (it bounced around the networks until 1971). Neither was Berle the first personality whom television transformed into a star; Howdy Doody had bowed in late 1947, almost a full year before the 'Texaco Star Theatre' hit the waves. Berle, however, was the first TV superstar. As with Amos 'n' Andy on radio, restaurateurs and moving-picture theater managers would notice a drop in

business when the 'Star Theatre' was broadcast. People bought television sets to watch 'Uncle Miltie,' and he justly earned thereby the encomium 'Mr Television.' NBC, believing that his star, if not his 'Star Theatre,' would never fade, awarded him a 30-year contract. In fact, the 'Texaco Star Theatre' ended in 1953, followed by two formats of a 'Milton Berle Show' variety hour. By the end of the Golden Age, he was the host of 'Jackpot Bowling.' Except by way of a few flickering kinescopes, it is nearly impossible to appreciate the madcap verve – and the impact – that Milton

PREVIOUS SPREAD: *Sid Caesar and Imogene Coca. If Berle was 'Mr Television,' they were the First Family, reigning on* Your Show of Shows.

OPPOSITE TOP: *Milton Berle – 'Uncle Miltie,' here shown with Vivian Blaine – dominated Americans' Tuesday nights during the early Golden Age.*

OPPOSITE BOTTOM: *A shooting set of* Texaco Star Theatre *with Berle in drag, as he often appeared. Television could make small stages seem large.*

LEFT: *Celebrities scrambled to appear on the* Texaco Star Theatre; *Berle is shown with guest Slapsie Maxie Rosenbloom.*

BELOW: *The king of early Golden Age television, Milton Berle.*

Berle generated when the Golden Age of television dawned.

The 'Star Theatre' was mostly comedy, but earned its variety label by offering music and dance as well. With Berle as permanent host, it made its debut on 8 June 1948. Less than two weeks later, another institution was born – a program that packed more light variety into its format than any show before or since: 'The Toast of the Town.' If Berle revived burlesque, then 'Toast' host Ed Sullivan reincarnated the legitimate stage and Palace- or Paladium-type variety performance.

TOP: Berle commanded international stars (and the finest gowns), as here with Jean Sablon, Victor Moore and Gracie Fields.

ABOVE: Berle in a skit with Ethel Merman, and RIGHT as Cleopatra.

A former sports reporter on The New York *Graphic*, a racy tabloid of the 1920s, Sullivan graduated to the New York *News* as Broadway gossip columnist, his paper's answer to Walter Winchell. Although his show originally featured a chorus line and a troupe of dancers, eventually (by the time it became simply 'The Ed Sullivan Show' in 1955) Sullivan would merely introduce acts and let them do their things. In truth, this was Sullivan at his best, for during the incredible 23-year run of his showcase he never seemed comfortable on screen, and was certainly never smooth or telegenic. His mannerisms were nervous, his speech awkward, his introductions laced with malaprops. Yet he produced programs of dizzying variety: classical pianists and dog acts; Shakespearean declamations and trained seals; the Bolshoi Ballet and Topo Gigio, the talking Italian mouse who always upstaged the bumbling Sullivan. He also gave America the first national views of Elvis Presley and The Beatles.

America usually likes its heroes handsomer and smoother than the average man, and never more so than in the television age. But television has also created the 'personality,' someone who is about as homely and awkward as the next guy and seems to manifest no particular talents for dancing, singing, or acting. Ed Sullivan was the first of this unique group, and in his way he defined the flavor of television variety shows for a generation.

At the end of 1948, another radio star shifted to television with another program of amateur acts. 'Arthur Godfrey's Talent Scouts' helped discover such talents as the McGuire Sisters and Patsy Cline, and solidified the already-popular Godfrey with a new audience. His relaxed manner, folksy and full of chuckles, was in direct contrast to that of the brash Berle, as it became evident that the small screen could also be the conduit of an intimate ambience. Godfrey chatted about his sponsors instead of pitching their products loudly, and the red-haired, freckled host would impulsively produce his ukelele to sing little ditties. The mild-mannered man of the ubiquitous 'How are ya, how are ya?' was not so mild-mannered behind the scenes, where his staff feuds made fan-publication headlines with regularity. He fired Julius LaRosa on the air for 'lacking humility,' saying 'Thank you Julie . . . and that, folks, was Julie's swan song.'

During one period Godfrey had three network shows running simultaneously. Besides 'Talents Scouts,' he hosted 'Arthur Godfrey and Friends' (a variety hour of the now-typical television kind) and 'Arthur Godfrey Time,'

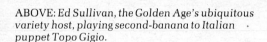

ABOVE: *Ed Sullivan, the Golden Age's ubiquitous variety host, playing second-banana to Italian puppet Topo Gigio.*

LEFT: *Two Golden Age superstars, Ed Sullivan and Sid Caesar.*

BELOW: *A low-key host of Golden Age variety programs, Arthur Godfrey.*

a four-day-a-week daytime show of talk and variety acts.

There was one more classic program of the pioneer variety shows. It had a star, but its success was due to a full, talented ensemble. More, a gifted producer and astounding crew of writers – all fully credited – combined for one of the finest packages of the Golden Age. 'The Admiral Broadway Revue' made its debut on 28 December 1949, produced by Max Liebman. It was instantly popular with critics and viewers – so popular, legend has it, that Admiral withdrew its sponsorship after 17 weeks because it could not manufacture TV sets fast enough to meet the demand generated by its program. Strictly true or not, the next step was taken by the NBC executive and genius Sylvester 'Pat' Weaver, who invited Liebman to repeat his formula every week as part of the network's 'Saturday Night Review.' Liebman agreed to do 90 minutes a week, and so did the stars, Sid Caesar and Imogene Coca.

The series, of course, was eventually renamed 'Your Show of Shows' and was seized upon as an inspired work of comedy-variety by the whole nation. The program featured many comedy skits and what appeared to be wild improvisation (there was ad-libbing, but the entire program was under tight creative control). Caesar was the Man of a Thousand Accents, and Miss Coca was a comedienne of astonishing virtuosity. Carl Reiner, one of the writers, and Howard Morris were ensemble players who added to the manic, madcap flavor. Among the recurring zany characters portrayed were novelist Somerset Winterset, Professor von Wolfgang and Doris and Charlie Hickenlooper.

No less inspired than the performers were the writers on 'Your Show of Shows,' a list of whom could proudly fill a corridor in a comedy Hall of Fame: Reiner, Mel Brooks, Neil Simon, Woody Allen, Larry Gelbart (later the force behind M*A*S*H) and Selma Diamond.

Sid Caesar staked a new claim in his various shows that ran into 1958. While Berle was adapting vaudeville humor, and Sullivan made television the new location of legit variety, Caesar proved that television could be an originator of consistent, quality ensemble humor. What Liebman and his crew produced with such dizzying frequency was the comedic counterpart of the excellent live dramas that were dominating TV schedules and impressing viewers as well as critics.

As Berle, Sullivan, Godfrey, and Caesar experimented with themes, Pat Weaver at NBC was experimenting with formats. He suspected that a late-night

LEFT: *Sid Caesar, who first hit television stardom as host of* The Admiral Broadway Revue *on the combined East-West networks of NBC and DuMont.*

BELOW: On Your Show of Shows, *the brilliant ensemble of Howard Morris, Caesar, Imogene Coca and Carl Reiner held forth.*

BOTTOM: *Caesar played a variety of characters in all types of skits in the comedy/variety* Your Show of Shows, *produced by Max Liebman.*

OPPOSITE TOP: *After* Your Show of Shows, *Sid Caesar and Imogene Coca hosted separate variety programs before teaming again in 1958.*

OPPOSITE BOTTOM: Coca and Caesar – perfect comic foils for each other, perfectly suited for brash, improvisational, innovative Golden Age comedy.

variety program could be a success, but it was a relatively untested concept that met widespread scepticism. Weaver and the insomniacs finally won out, although the format was slow to take off. Jan Murray was invited to host such a variety show, but declined. Creesh Hornsby accepted, but contracted a fatal disease and died the weekend before the NBC program's debut. Tex McCrary and Jinx Falkenburg (he a witty ad man, she a former Miss America) proved too laconic for the tube when they served as guest hosts. Wally Cox was too withdrawn, and Martin & Lewis were – predictably – too brash, especially after Jerry Lewis succeeded in finally breaking a sponsor's 'unbreakable' glass on the air. Finally, Weaver looked into his Casting Book under the Berle-type category and came up with Jerry Lester. The chemistry worked.

In fact, Jerry Lester could sometimes make Berle look distinguished. He was a relatively obscure baggy-pants comedian who did unpredictable things, mugged outrageously, milked laughs, and generally slapsticked his audience into getting their money's worth of sleeplessness. 'Broadway Open House' – the late-night show's title – featured an ensemble that included Dagmar, a chesty blonde who lent an air of 'Dr Krankheit' to every sketch she joined. The diminutive Lester came up to her cleavage – and he did so as frequently as he could.

'Broadway Open House' aired three times a week, with Morey Amsterdam providing his brand of lunacy and music on the other two nights between eleven o'clock and midnight. Wayne Howell and Milton DeLugg were the announcer and bandleader, respectively, on 'Broadway Open House,' creating two permanent second-banana slots that would survive into the years after it became NBC's 'Tonight Show.'

The fledgling DuMont Network was determined not to be outdone by the rash of live variety shows. It latched on to one of television's most inspired comedians and variety-show hosts, Jackie Gleason. Many might not have predicted a meteoric career for the movie comic: his performances in 'The Life of Riley,' while workmanlike, gave no hint of the incredible variety of comic personae he could assume, or the brilliant creativity he would manifest in the hour-long variety classics that would span three decades on television.

'The Cavalcade of Stars' was the title of Gleason's variety show on DuMont in 1950 – two years later it switched to CBS as 'The Jackie Gleason Show' – and it was filled to the brim with unforgettable skits and characters, including 'The Honeymooners,' with Pert Kelton as wife Alice Kramden.

On CBS, with larger budgets, Gleason let loose his full creativity. He was a veteran comedian well before television, and his characters – bus driver Ralph Kramden, loudmouth Charlie Bracken, tipsy Reginald Van Gleason III, the wimpy Poor Soul – provided opportunities for brilliant virtuoso performances. Gleason was also an accomplished conductor-arranger (although he maintained that he couldn't read music) and occasionally brought sophisticated 'music for lovers only' to his hour. And, as his superb dramatic performances on television and in the movies would prove, Gleason had sensitivity; his performances, even the farces, were under-

ABOVE: Broadway Open House *aired the first late-night variety/talk-show; shown are Dagmar, host Jerry Lester and bandleader Milton DeLugg.*

RIGHT: *The Great One – Jackie Gleason.*

pinned by a depth of understanding.

Gleason was also blessed with fine writers and one of the finest comedy casts in the history of television. Audrey Meadows, late of the 'Bob and Ray Show,' was a comedienne whose main role was wife Alice in the Honeymooners segments, which were the high points of the Gleason show and which took off as a series in 1955. She offered a fine comic touch in both humorous and poignant moments. Art Carney played Ed Norton in the Honeymooners sketches and various other character roles, proving himself a gifted comedic talent. During the Golden Age he also performed in several acclaimed TV specials, (including 'Harvey,' 'Burlesque' and 'Charlie's Aunt') and later won an Oscar (in 'Harry and Tonto').

RIGHT: Among Gleason's later rep players was vocalist/comedian Frank Fontaine. Gleason was a respected composer and bandleader, and was responsible for reuniting the Dorsey Brothers.

BELOW: Jackie Gleason in his famous pose – 'And away we go!'

BELOW CENTER: Reggie Van Gleason III, the insouciant drunk, was one of The Great One's personae.

BELOW LOWER RIGHT: The Poor Soul was another Gleason character – a pantomimic, pudgy Casper Milquetoast.

OPPOSITE PAGE: Yet another character of Gleason was Charlie Bracken, the loudmouth. Gleason performed all sorts of physical comedy, and once broke his ankle on-camera.

As every strata in the lode of American comedic tradition was mined, Red Skelton, a masterful clown, brought his 'Red Skelton Show' to television and made it an instant hit. He featured many guests, and a true varietal mix of songs and skits, but the real stars were the many character types Skelton played: his best sketches were in costume, as Gertrude and Heathcliff, the seagulls; Sherriff Deadeye, the cowboy; The Mean Widdle Kid, a brat in Buster-Brown costume; and Clem Kadiddlehopper, the country hick. Skelton also appeared often, and appropriately, as a traditional circus clown in farcical but poignant bits that delighted audiences through the 1971 season. Every program would close with a personal chat on stage with his studio audience and a sincere 'Good night . . . God Bless!'

Art Linkletter hosted a variety program for ABC from 1950-52 ('Life with Linkletter'), but that was not the main vehicle of his television contribution. In 1952 he switched to CBS for an afternoon variety show that featured children and catered to housewives, 'Art Linkletter's House Party.' It was a successful formula and owed a great deal to Linkletter's smooth ad-libbing and rapport with nonprofessional guests. Two years later, for a third network, came the game show 'People Are Funny,' hosted by Linkletter on NBC in a series that was simultaneous with 'House Party.'

The Golden Age was producing radio stars who made an easy transition to television, and obscure talents from the stage and screen who found their metier on the tube. But the first individual who was completely a product of the television age was also – at the time and ever since – arguably its greatest talent. Ernie Kovacs, a product of local shows in Trenton, New Jersey, and Philadelphia, hit the networks in 1950 with his totally individual sense of humor – wry, satiric, surrealistic – and an overwhelming mastery of TV's limitations and potentialities.

He deftly skirted the limitations, and decades before MTV and computerized effects, stretched the language and syntax of visual and aural communication on the small screen, playing with its conventions and with viewers' perceptions. He was offbeat enough – *very* offbeat – to be bounced from show to show during the 1950s, but he was brilliant enough to be constantly working. 'Deadline for Dinner' was a satire on DuMont in 1950, a format transferred to NBC in the daytime 'Kovacs on the Corner' the next year. In 1951 'It's Time for Ernie' and 'Ernie in Kovacsland' also ran. Later shows included 'Kovacs Unlimited,' 'The Kovacs Show,' and 'The

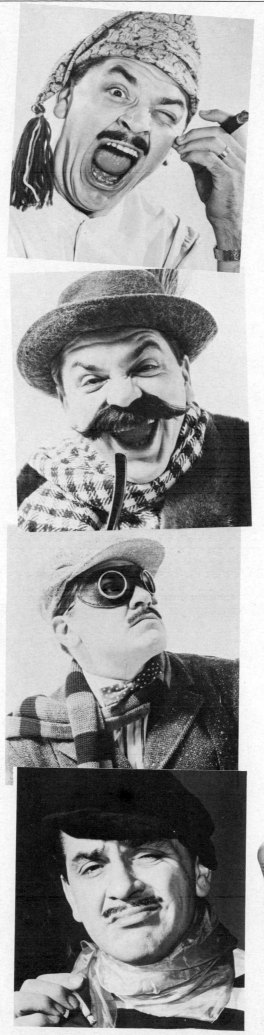

New Ernie Kovacs Show.' He also hosted a quiz show, 'Take a Good Look,' that was as much a spoof of quiz shows as a game in itself. And in 1955 Kovacs was a host of the 'Tonight Show.'

Kovacs exercised complete creative control of his programs. There was no other way the television establishment would have allowed – or conceived of – occasional half-hours with absolutely no dialogue, or the bizarre use of visual tricks like water pouring sideways. Kovacs used stop-action film and video tape to create lunatic sequences. Like other television comics, he compiled his own cast of characters, including Percy Dovetonsils, poet; Wolfgang Sauerbraten; Pierre Ragout; Irving Wong; and the bizarre Nairobi Trio, a group of musical, mechanical simians. It was a major loss to the medium when Kovacs died in an auto crash in 1961 after leaving a christening party at a friend's house. At a time when television was allowing others to be iconoclasts of content, Kovacs was an iconoclast of forms and their parameters. Others in the future may stretch to his levels of innovation, but none can surpass his inventiveness and creative *élan*.

OPPOSITE: *Red Skelton, the Golden Age's most beloved clown, as Clem Kadiddlehopper; with guest Bobby Rydell, a fifties rocker.*

LEFT, TOP TO BOTTOM: *Four of the many alteregos of the Golden Age genius Ernie Kovacs. More than his characters, his approach and technical innovations broke new ground in television's syntax.*

BELOW: *Art Linkletter.*

Steve Allen emerged at the same time as Kovacs. His brand of non-conformist humor and unconventional behavior was close to Kovacs', and the two were definitely soul-mates of comedy, but Allen was more structured and therefore more commercial. Allen should not be compared to Kovacs – nobody should be – but rather to other variety-show hosts and talk-show masters. Those were Allen's chosen fields, and against all comers Steve Allen was, and remains, the most interesting, best informed, least inhibited of them all.

Allen was trained on radio, where he developed his open, improvisational style of ad libs, off-the-cuff humor, and interplay with the audience. He graduated to guest spots on network game shows, where his literate wit served him well, and he finally hosted a quiz show himself – 'Songs for Sale.' In quick succession he hosted a nightly hour on CBS (in 1951) and a noontime daily program. In 1953, when Jerry Lester's 'Broadway Open House' petered out, Steve Allen took over, first on a show that withdrew to NBC's New York affiliate solely, and then, the following year, on the full network between 11:30 PM and 1:00 AM.

The television humor of Steve Allen, a certified genius, was no less physical than Lester's but it was more cerebral. What was not strictly intellectual (puns, literal humor, irony) was wonderfully silly, as when he attached thousands of tea bags to himself and was dunked into a vat of warm water by a crane as the World's Largest Tea Bag. Other routines were telephone-related: Allen would answer want ads in out-of-town papers, or call numbers at random from phone books, conducting crazed conversations while the audience listened. Occasionally, he would position cameras on unknowing passersby outside the studio, and provide silly voices for unsuspecting pedestrians. His lack of inhibition extended to his demeanor, as he literally rolled on the floor laughing at some piece of foolery, whether his own or a guest's. His interviews and conversations were peppered with non sequiturs like 'Schmock! Schmock!' and 'How's your fern?', and his desk (he was the first talk-show host to include such furniture as a prop) was littered with noise-makers, whistles, bells, and the ever-present glass of orange juice.

Steve Allen's lunacy was inspired, and on the more serious side he wrote thousands of pieces of music ('This Could Be the Start of Something Big' and 'Gravy Train Waltz' are two of his most famous) and several books. He also

LEFT: *Steve Allen, the most cerebral of the Golden Age's late-night talk-show hosts, reinforces his image while posing with Diana Dors.*

ABOVE: *Even commercials became fodder for Allen humor . . . and sponsors loved the extra attention. Seen here is Allen and announcer Gene Rayburn, onetime radio host and future game show emcee.*

LEFT: *Multi-talented Steve Allen was not chary of highlighting other comedians and talents. He is shown here with two of his most prominent sidemen, Don Knotts (left) and Louis Nye (right).*

BELOW: *Steve Allen was comedian, composer, author, musician, and sometimes dancer.*

engaged in political activity and developed a program of historical speculation for the Public Broadcasting System ('Meeting of the Minds'). For all of his overwhelming talent, Allen surrounded himself with a large group of comedic sidemen and shared the spotlight, the laughs, and the credit with them. His discoveries included Tom Posten (who, in man-in-the-street interviews, would be the guy who forgot his own name); Don Knotts (always playing an extremely nervous fellow); Louis Nye ('Hi-ho, Steverino!'); Dayton Allen (no relation to Steve, he always asked 'Why not?'); Bill Dana (who played the character José Jimenez); and Steve Lawrence and Eydie Gorme. Allen Sherman was one of Steve Allen's writers: he became a celebrity performer himself, with deadpan-delivery satiric songs based on classical melodies.

After Steve Allen left the 'Tonight Show' (to devote his time to an hour-long variety program on Sundays that competed with Ed Sullivan and 'Maverick'), NBC attempted a late-night melange hosted by Jack Lescoulie and featuring newspaper columnists from around the country. Titled 'Tonight: America After Dark,' it began in January of 1957 and flopped in half a year's time. It seemed that the single-host, talk-and-variety format was best after all, and a new host was found in a television journeyman, a veteran of several variety shows and quiz programs. Jack Paar was that host, and he brought a new style to the genre. Although singing, comedy and various acts qualified his programs for the variety label, Paar's specialty was conversation; his was the first series that could consistently be termed a talk show. Besides guests who passed through, Paar signed up a large number of regulars whose conversation routinely – and conveniently – ran to the eccentric and outrageous. The typical Paar chat would feature one guest who uttered unpredictable and extreme statements (Alexander King was one such regular), or 'naive' transplanted foreigners who feigned malapropisms (like French chanteuse Genevieve or Jack Douglas's Japanese wife).

Other familiar faces on Jack Paar's 'Tonight Show' (later called 'The Jack Paar Show') were Cliff Arquette (as Charlie Weaver), Pat Harrington, Jr (as Guido Panzini), Peggy Cass, Mary Margaret McBride, Dodie Goodman, Oscar Levant, Elsa Maxwell and the Bill Baird Puppets. The most prominent eccentric personality was Paar's own: He proudly wore his heart on his sleeve and regularly wept on camera, whether over Walter Winchell's snipes in newspaper columns, or network interference in his productions (he boycotted his own series when the network standards-and-practices department deleted the word 'toilet' from one of his jokes).

Jack Paar was a very personal type of variety-show host — the audience could feel as if he were talking to each of them ('I kid you not' was one of his catch-phrases). Although he appeared very soft-spoken and reserved, it is the mark of extreme extroversion to display private emotions publicly and to assume that every viewer shared — or cared. For a long time the viewers did seem to care, enjoying Paar's unique, individual brand of television. Then he walked off once too often and, in 1962, after a revolving-door of guest hosts, NBC settled on Johnny Carson to host the 'Tonight Show.' Gone were Jack Paar's traps and trappings, forever suspended in the Golden Age (he later attempted some prime-time variety programs that failed), and gone too were network objections to jokes about toilets; Carson ushered in a style that ended any coyness about the double-entendre.

Hosts may have come and gone, but NBC was supreme in the late-night time slot. Similarly, it dominated a strange period that had previously been thought undesirable — and uncommercial — by the networks. The slot was early-morning, and the man who forged a new television genre, once again, was Pat Weaver, programmer at NBC. Weaver was constantly thinking of diverse formats by which to make the medium evergreen to viewers ('Wide Wide World,' and 'Home,' a daily magazine, were two experiments). With 'Today' — broadcast from 7:00 to 9:00 AM, during breakfast, Weaver found a durable format.

'Today' was variety of the most eclectic sort. Occasionally, the networks would pretend that their early-morning shows were primarily news programs, but news was always but a small percentage of the larger show, compartmentalized via introductions and special sets. (When CBS fielded a competitor, Walter Cronkite, he regularly chatted with comedic puppets, diminishing the hard-news aura.) 'Today' offered news, information (how-to segments and soft features), interviews with celebrities, time checks, weather around the nation, sports and women's features such as fashion. There were 'editors' for the various categories (Barbara Walters, daughter of nightclub owner Lou Walters, became hostess of the program) and a lively mix of changing foci and sets.

The anchor of the 'Today' show (in terms of ballast-like stability as well as title) was Dave Garroway, a low-keyed former host of a local Chicago variety show. Garroway couldn't sing or dance or do comedy skits, but he made the audience comfortable and served as an

amiable ringleader of all the diverse segments around him on the morning show. Somewhat intellectual in mien, with bow tie, glasses, and a deliberate conversational style, Garroway lent a relaxed, confident air to the program during its formative years (1952-61), after which he left. There was hard news, and there were softer features, but during Garroway's reign segments were softer yet: there were occasional appearances by chimpanzee J Fred Muggs, who had the run of the studio, including guests' chairs and the host's lap.

OPPOSITE: *The low-key, mercurial Jack Paar featured an ensemble of chatty personalities on* The Tonight Show. *He sits between two of his most memorable guests, Genevieve and Cliff Arquette (Charlie Weaver).*

ABOVE: *Johnny Carson, veteran of many shows and formats during the Golden Age, eventually succeeded Paar. He is seen here shilling Rudy Vallee's book with the crooner.*

BELOW: *Urbane Dave Garroway provided* The Today Show *its flavor, and J Fred Muggs tried to periodically sabotage the host's best efforts.*

Other regulars on 'Today' were Jack Lescoulie (sports); Charles Van Doren (features, before he became anathema to television by perjuring himself during the quiz-show scandals); Betsy Palmer (women's features); and Frank Blair (news).

Not all the variety shows of the Golden Age were comedy- or chat-oriented, of course. The musical variety series was a staple from the start, giving viewers with small sets the extravagant feel of lavish Broadway productions and international stars. Television could be all things to all people; while one of its inherent specialties was the intimate aura of close-ups and live drama, it also eventually offered long shots and entertainment spectacles. Although visual details may have looked muddy at first, the music of big orchestras and choruses – the very scope of it all – covered a multitude of dins.

There were several superstars of musical variety whose manners and program chemistry were perfect for the new medium. With different musical guests every week, they were able to blend their own song stylings with inevitable comedy routines into offerings that were simultaneously familiar and fresh. Perry Como was the epitome of such a host. His soft voice and somnabulent style did not prevent him from being a strong television presence, an appealing on-air personality. He started his small-screen career in 1948 on 'The Chesterfield Supper Club' and earned 'The Perry Como Show' two years later, for a while as a 15-minute, several-times-a-week spot and finally as a ratings-dominant weekly musical-variety program.

Dinah Shore, a pop singer from Tennessee, was the hostess of a musical-variety show that alternated with Como's in the early 1950s. She, too, earned her own weekly show (after a series of highly rated specials) and her program for Chevrolet, closing with her patented big kiss thrown to the audience, was a long-running favorite. Miss Shore proved adept at comedy, too, and in later years took on a new role as hostess of a popular syndicated daytime talk show.

TOP RIGHT: *Somnambulent Perry Como and perky Dinah Shore each hosted popular musical/variety shows of the Golden Age.*

RIGHT: *The cast of* Your Hit Parade *in 1952, before rock 'n' roll hastened the demise of such pop shows.*

OPPOSITE, TOP: *Garry Moore, Dorothy Loudon and Durwood Kirby of The Garry Moore Show. Carol Burnett was also a featured performer.*

OPPOSITE, BOTTOM: *Jimmy Durante – star of vaudeville, speakeasies, radio, movies . . . and television.*

'Your Hit Parade' began in 1950, another crossover from radio, and remained throughout the Golden Age, although it coped awkwardly with the rock 'n' roll onslaught in the later 1950s. The weekly show featured performances of the top-charted records, and its first host included Snooky Lanson and Dorothy Collins; other hosts included June Valli and Gisele MacKenzie. 'Kay Kyser's College of Musical Knowledge' was another radio crossover, a variety-and-quiz based on familiar songs and tunes. The vaudeville comic Ish Kabbible played saxophone in the band, and Mike Douglas, later host of his own talk show, was a featured vocalist. In 1954, upon Kyser's retirement, Tennessee Ernie Ford became host. Ford – with a crackerbarrel wit and handsome baritone stylings – had risen through country music (and Los Angeles television's pioneer 'Hometown Jamboree' hosted by Cliffie Stone) to become a pop star of wide appeal. His cover version of Merle Travis's 'Sixteen Tons' was one of the 1950s' major records. During the Golden Age, Ford hosted both daily programs and weekly series of music and variety after his stint on the 'College of Musical Knowledge'; he also did guest comedy spots on major series like 'The Lucy-Desi Comedy Hour.' Ford closed each of his variety shows with a gospel song, calling religious numbers 'the greatest love songs of them all.'

Jimmy Durante was a nightclub and movie personality to whom television provided a new lease on a colorful career. A veteran of performances in his own speakeasies during Prohibition, movies during the 1930s, and a radio show in the 1940s, Durante's brand of old songs, comic mugging, and assaults on the English language made him a memorable host of musical-variety programs. He regularly teamed colleagues from his days in vaudeville (like his nightclub partner Eddie Jackson) with contemporary newcomers (like the Lennon Sisters, whom he made his summer replacements one season) for a fresh mixture. He closed each show with a melancholy walk away from the camera along lighted circles on the floor after his ritual farewell to his late wife: 'Good night, Mrs Calabash, wherever you are.' Durante's series included 'The Buick Circus Hour,' 'The Texaco Star Theatre,' and 'The Jimmy Durante Show.'

Garry Moore was another variety-show host who demonstrated that a high-pressure personality was not a requisite for a successful reception. He hosted a daytime variety program and later was master of ceremonies (emcee, in TV parlance) of the popular game show 'I've Got a Secret.' But his greatest fame came with the weekly musical-variety series 'The Garry Moore Show,' famed for the ensemble players the diminutive Moore gathered around him. Included were Durwood Kirby and Marion Lorne, wonderful character comics, and a singing, dancing, rubber-faced comedienne adept at physical humor and farce named Carol Burnett. She later reprised the basic format, with her own comedy ensemble, in the acclaimed 'Carol Burnett Show' of the 1960s and '70s.

Country music found a reasonably warm reception on network television, considering the industry's devotion to Northern urban markets. 'The Grand Ole Opry,' from the country-music shrine in Nashville, and the 'Ozark Jubilee' from Springfield, Missouri (hosted by Red Foley and later called 'Jubilee USA') offered the biggest names in the field in variety formats. Pee Wee King and Eddy Arnold had network shows, and Ernest Tubb and Porter Wagoner had syndicated programs. Jimmy Dean hosted a music-and-talk show in the mornings on a local Washington, DC, station and was boosted to network television by the appeal of his trademark folksiness. Pat Boone (a pop singer who was the son-in-law of Red Foley) hosted a popular variety series when his hit records and brand of soft-rock made him an antiseptic alternative

to the Elvises of the entertainment world.

Two all-musical programs made their debuts in the mid-1950s. Lawrence Welk hosted the 'Dodge Dancing Party' in 1955 (the title referred to the automotive sponsor, not a style of dancing), which catered increasingly to the geriatric set. Older dances, older tunes, older memories, and older theme segments appealed to a sizeable audience immune to excessive schmaltz. Welk had many trademarks: champagne bubbles floating around his band; a bizarre accent (it pervaded every word,

although he had been born in America); and oft-repeated phrases like the kickoff 'Ah-one, ah-two . . .' and, after each number by the band, ''Thenk you boysss.' Another trademark was his large and loyal following; when ABC dropped 'The Lawrence Welk Show' in 1971, he immediately signed up more stations in syndication than the network

had on its own string. (The same thing happened with 'Hee Haw,' and Roy Clark recorded a song celebrating the irony: 'The Lawrence Welk–Hee Haw–Counter-Revolutionary Polka.') Among the many featured singers and musicians on 'Lawrence Welk' – and it was long-rumored that he would hire only Catholics – were the Lennon Sisters, Pete Fountain, Myron Floren, Jo Ann Castle and the Hotsy Totsy Boys.

Two years after Welk's network debut, in 1957, 'American Bandstand' went national. The rock 'n' roll showcase was broadcast from Philadelphia (whence it originated in 1952) and its second host was Dick Clark; its first host had been fired after he received a drunk-driving citation during his station's Road Safety campaign. 'American Bandstand' featured virtually every major and many minor acts in rock since the music had erupted in the mid-1950s. It also showcased the major dance steps – and rated individual dance-floor performances. The music itself was never rated, but 'American Bandstand' transformed the trick of lip-synching to a fine art.

Of all the services provided by 'American Bandstand' to popular culture, perhaps the most notable, if unheralded, is the preservation and acceptance of the rock sound in establishment quarters despite its prevailing bad-boy image, payola scandals, and other troubles of the times. Clark continued to host 'Bandstand' even after he parlayed its success into an amazing personal empire as game-show host and producer of television series and specials.

Another much-loved emcee of the early days was singer Kate Smith, whose popular variety series included 'The Kate Smith Hour.' Other emcees were aired daily in the late afternoon (Monday through Friday). Ken Murray (who switched from vaudeville to hosting specials based on his 'home movies' of Hollywood celebrities); Rosemary Clooney ('Songs for Sale'); Frank Sinatra (who tried and failed in two network variety series); Martha Raye; and Pinky Lee (who starred in his own show and 'Those Two' with Vivian Blaine). The ex-burlesque comic also hosted a children's program. Alan Young had a popular musical-variety show bearing

OPPOSITE, TOP: *Carol Burnett, comedienne extraordinaire, as Calamity Jane.*

OPPOSITE, BOTTOM: *Red Foley's Ozark Jubilee was one of many popular Golden Age country-music programs.*

ABOVE: *Lawrence Welk, sans bubbles.*

LEFT: *Perennial teen Dick Clark on* American Bandstand.

his name, and other early variety shows included 'Jane Frohman's USA Canteen,' 'The Dennis Day Show,' 'The Bob Hope Show' – before he 'retired' to do specials and film shows at overseas military bases several times a year – 'The George Gobel show,' 'The Ed Wynn Show,' 'The Sam Levenson Show' (more a program of schmooze and chat than song and dance), and the 'Saturday Night Revue,' which, apart from the Sid Caesar segment, sometimes originated in Chicago and featured rotating hosts, including Jack Carter, Hoagy Carmichael, Alan Young, Ben Blue and Eddie Albert.

Once television was established, it seemed that every star from every era was on the tube, in complex production numbers with full complements of musicians, singers and dancers. Olsen and Johnson had their own variety series in 1949, 'Fireball Fun for All.' Among other stars who had their own variety series were Henny Youngman and Rocky Graziano ('The Henny and Rocky Show'); Doodles Weaver; Red Buttons; Jonathan Winters (squarely in the round mold of Ernie Kovacs and Steve Allen); Faye Emerson; Arlene Francis; Wendy Barrie; Carmel Myers; Robert Q Lewis; Morton Downey; Lilli Palmer; Will Rogers Jr; and Sherman Billingsley with his 'Stork Club' interviews.

One of the hallmarks of early television was the anthology variety show – truly re-creating the tradition of the grand variety spectacles on stage – which featured rotating hosts, or simply a surprise host every week. By the later 1950s, this sort of series had almost disappeared; not only were variety shows in general decline, but, as with the comedy shows and the transition from live to episodic drama, television's corporate masters recognized the cult of personality. It was better in their eyes to let the public attach itself to a performer; such loyalty was firmer than that to a title or a time slot. Among the early great variety anthologies was 'The Colgate Comedy Hour,' whose emcees included Eddie Cantor, Abbott and Costello, Martin and Lewis, Donald O'Connor and Judy Canova. Some of television's finest moments of elaborate comedy-and-music were on the 'Colgate' show. 'Four Star Revue,' later titled 'All-Star Revue,' featured as hosts Olsen and Johnson, Jimmy Durante, Danny Thomas, Victor Borge, Martha Raye, George Jessel, the Ritz Brothers and Ed Wynn. 'Showtime USA' featured scenes from Broadway comedies and musicals and was hosted by Henry Fonda.

Interestingly, a pioneer of jazz was also a pioneer of music on television. Paul Whiteman, who brought jazz to Carnegie Hall and to radio, was host of 'The Goodyear Revue' and, improbably, 'The TV Teen Club.' He also served as ABC's early vice president for musical affairs. Fred Waring and His Pennsylvanians also had their own musical-variety show, and other personalities in the genre included Horace Heidt, Bob Crosby (Bing's brother, whose band, the Bobcats, had brought Boogie-Woogie to Swing), Spike Jones and His City Slickers (the one band on television that was intentionally funny), Ray Anthony, and Meredith Willson, who hosted a Sunday night program of music years before he wrote and scored Broadway's legendary 'Music Man.'

Nat King Cole, a former virtuoso jazz pianist, brought his ultra-smooth pop vocal stylings to network television in 1956. He was backed by Nelson Riddle and had the biggest names in show business as his guests. But lack of sponsorship due to opposition in some markets because Cole was black led to the cancellation of the 'Nat King Cole Show' after one season on NBC in 1956-57.

Ford sponsored notable series and specials in variety during the Golden Age. On 'Ford Star Jubilee' there was Judy Garland's memorable television debut in a variety spectacular. On 'Ford Startime,' there were presentations hosted by Rosalind Russell, Dean Martin, George Burns and Ethel Merman.

OPPOSITE, TOP: *Bob Hope became a seemingly permanent fixture on American television, from telethons to specials to annual USO-servicemen's shows. Here the 'Nose' emulates the 'Lip,' Maurice Chevalier.*

OPPOSITE, BOTTOM: *Bing Crosby, Hope's screen partner, also had his own specials and series on television. This production number is from his 1954 show.*

LEFT: *George Gobel underplayed his comedy throughout the Golden Age. Here seen next to his British alter ego, Tootie Flimbone.*

BELOW: *Olsen and Johnson, the veteran comedy duo, also were early Golden Age series hosts.*

BOTTOM: *Fred Waring (second from left in a nostalgic skit) was a bandleader whose audience followed him to television.*

ABOVE: *Spike Jones and one of his unconventional soloists.*

CENTER, TOP: *Nat King Cole's first television success was DuMont's Harlem House.*

CENTER, BOTTOM: *Armstrong, Sinatra, Clooney and Crosby on 1957's Edsel Show.*

FAR RIGHT: *Frank Sinatra, Ethel Merman and Bert Lahr.*

Herb Shriner was the host of his own variety show, and so were Kay Starr, Patti Page ('The Big Record'), Gisele MacKenzie, Polly Bergen, Marge and Gower Champion, Betty White, Frances Langford and Don Ameche ('Startime') and Paul Winchell. With his puppets, Jerry Mahoney and Knucklehead Smiff, Winchell hosted both children's and adult variety programs through the 1950s.

Not all of television's music was pop and show stuff... but almost all. Leonard Bernstein's 'Young Peoples' Concerts' found a crack in the door for classical music, albeit during the Sunday-afternoon 'egghead' ghetto. 'The Bell Telephone Hour,' 'Meet the Masters,' and 'Voice of Firestone' also featured fine music, usually of the orchestral rather than the chamber variety.

Back on the finger-snapping side of the street, other variety programs included 'TV's Top Tunes' (with Peggy Lee and Mel Torme); 'The Johnny Dugan Show'; 'Mindy Carson Sings'; 'The Packard Showroom' with Martha Wright; 'Georgia Gibbs' Million Record Show'; 'Song Snapshots on a Summer Holiday' (starring Merv Griffin and Betty Ann Grove); 'Coke Time' with Eddie Fisher; 'The Chevy Showroom' (with Andy Williams, another Steve Allen discovery); 'Floor Show' (with Eddie Condon as host and jazz greats like Sidney Bechet and Wild Bill Davidson as guests); and 'The Florian ZaBach Show,' featuring the maestro of supper-club quality violin.

Other performers who hosted their own variety series included Billy Daniels, Tony Martin, Frankie Laine, Julius LaRosa, Patrice Munsel, John Raitt and Janet Blair, Guy Mitchell, Tony Bennett, Gordon MacRae, Sammy Kaye, Russ Morgan, Xavier Cugat and Jaye P Morgan. Miss Morgan, besides guesting on many musical shows, hosted her own variety series that featured her four brothers. Tommy and Jimmy Dorsey had their feud patched up by Jackie Gleason and then accepted half of his television hour in 1955 for their own show. ('The Honeymooners' as a series occupied the other 30 minutes). Elvis Presley made his tele-

vision debut on the Dorsey Brothers' show. 'Satins and Spurs,' formally billed as television's first spectacular, was a spectacular flop despite massive publicity. The Betty Hutton musical was a rare defeat for NBC's Pat Weaver and producer Max Liebman.

'Arthur Murray's Dance Party' featured the famed dancing instructor and his wife Kathryn in a potpourri of choreographed numbers, dancing instruction, contests and attempts at comedy routines. 'Dance Party' was a fixture throughout the 1950s, even through the rock 'n' roll era, during which Arthur and Kathryn waltzed to the bank. Another performer who 'cried all the way to the bank' was Liberace, who personified one of the new rules of the medium:

no matter how many detractors you have, they are still counted as legal viewers in the ratings. Older women swooned and younger men hooted as the prissy showman sat at the piano keyboard amid a barge-load of kitsch serving as props (candelabra, gaudy tuxedos, melon-sized rings) and tinkled out the schmaltz of 'light classics' and glissando-laden show tunes. Liberace's brother George, always dutifully introduced through a toothy smile, was forever standing behind the piano with a violin.

Perhaps the truest mix of variety – and the best – was found on 'Omnibus,' a tribute to truth in packaging. The series, hosted by Alistair Cooke, featured show tunes, scenes from Broadway and

classical productions, original drama, interviews, classical music, essays, poetry and much else during its run through the Golden Age. It was superb television and unfortunate only in its relatively lonely status.

But Cooke was only more eclectic, not more quality-conscious, than fellow producers during the 1950s. The majority of variety programs were committed to first-rate entertainment and top-flight talent. Viewers during the Golden Age of variety were provided with a feast. Even the programs that fell short of award-quality were at least earnest and spontaneous, making the genre, whether in comedy or musical categories, truly memorable and very entertaining.

The Golden Age of COMEDY

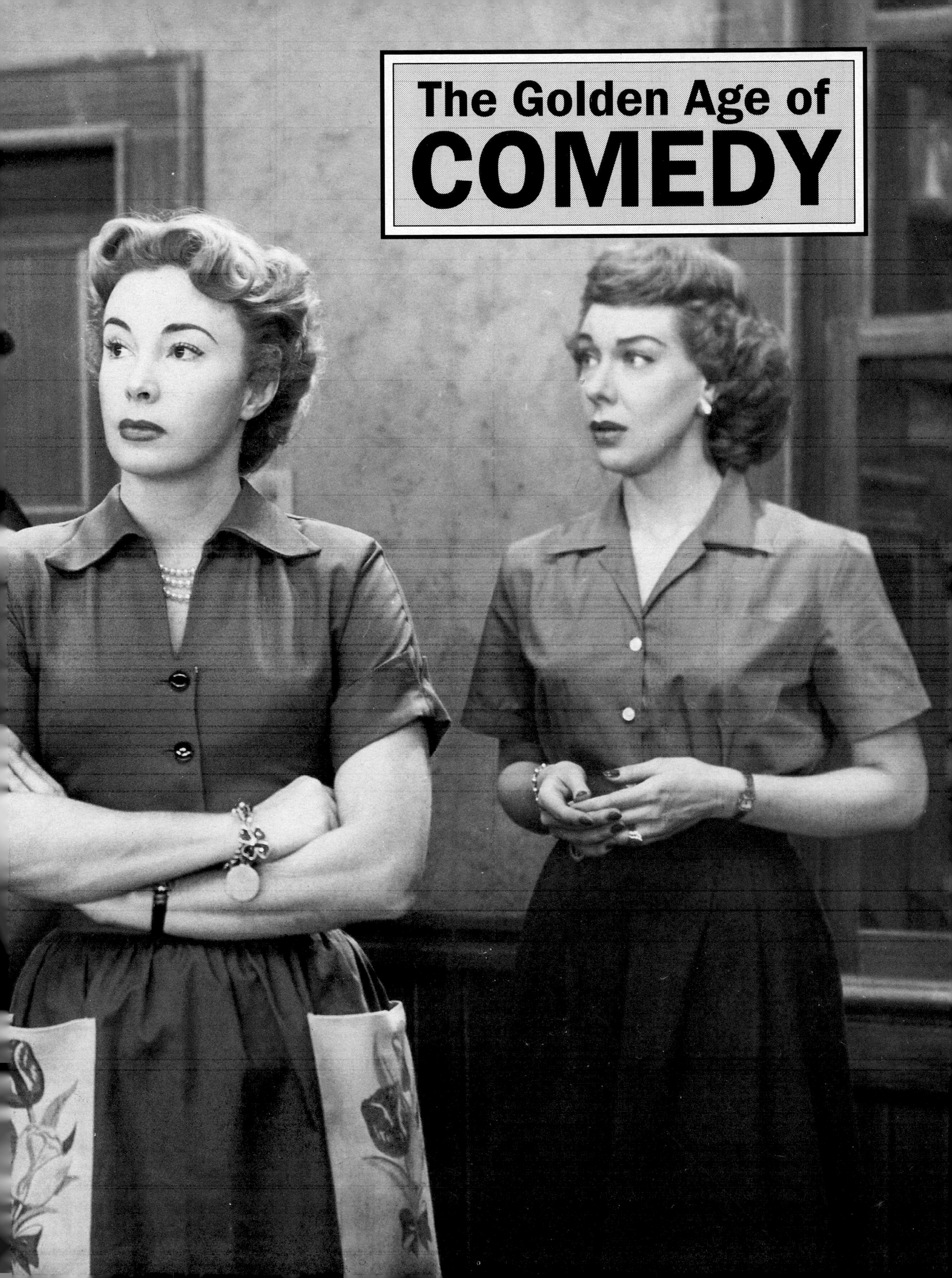

Viewer rapport was nowhere more magical than in the genre known as the sitcom – situation comedy. The success of 1950s comedy, however – not just situational, but also in variety and ensemble formats – can be credited to two sources.

The first factor in TV comedy's success in the Golden Age was, not surprisingly, the radio connection. Many programs, formats and stars transferred their activities from radio. When it became evident that television was here to stay and not a passing technological fad, the exodus from radio became a virtual stampede. Alistair Cooke, writing his weekly 'Letter from America' for the BBC in 1949, observed: 'The radio comedians, more than any other radio stars, appear ready to accept the fate they fear: the end of mass radio. Thereby they can help it come true. "All I know about television," said Bob Hope lately – and he spoke for legions in radio and the movies – "is, I want to get into it as soon as possible."'

So the comedians abandoned the medium that had nourished them for a generation – but it was part of natural selection and evolution in the entertainment arts. Radio, after all, had helped kill vaudeville. Now, on television, comedians like Ed Wynn could don their costumes and be visual again. Second bananas like Phil Silvers could become stars. Partially revealed personae like Lucille Ball's could be fulfilled. Geniuses whose work seemed appropriate *only* on television – Ernie Kovacs; Steve Allen; Kukla, Fran and Ollie – could find themselves.

Most importantly, many of the radio comedians who went to television – those who did not host comedy-variety shows, and those who were not the Kovacses of extreme experimentation – did not forsake everything. Many brought the characters, the formats, the writers that had made them hits on radio. And by carrying that baggage to the tube, radio comedians like Jack Benny, George Burns, Eve Arden and Gertude Berg ensured their success. The public could now *see* their favorites as well as hear them, and the stars engaged in a minimum of risk-taking by preserving their tested formulas. Best of all, a fledgling medium, in its first few years of full operation, could boast a list of the biggest-name stars in America.

The second factor in the success of television was the dominant format it happened to adopt. For all the Milton Berles and Sid Caesars with their variety, and the Ernie Kovacses and Kuklas with their intellectual drollery, it was the situation comedy that was to become the staple of Golden Age television.

The formula of the sitcom was simple and self-explanatory: a regular player would be caught in a situation and try, over the half-hour, to get free. In drama this is called Crisis and Resolution; in sitcoms it is called a prescription for laughs, with a couple of other ingredients thrown in. Almost always the player caught in the situation would have to be a bit daffy, else the situation and the problem would not arise. Further, because of the small screen and restricted time allotment, the humor had to be visual and basic.

Hence this genre – established on radio but honed for television – became a hallmark of the Golden Age of Television. Established stars, playing continuing characters (building viewer loyalty), involved themselves in short, visual, comedic situations. Not the least important were the writers who also migrated from radio: Al Capp once said that America's greatest humorists included an anonymous army of radio comedy writers, 'all named Nat and Sol,' who made the stars funny and kept the public laughing for years. Benny, Burns, Hope and the rest all brought

their writers with them to the tube.

Before the sitcom wave, however, the story should begin with a show referred to above. Its cast was barely human, its set a tiny stage, and its comedic situations more pixilated than any on television since. Burr Tillstrom was the creator and provider of voices, and Fran Allison was the hostess and only visible human on 'Kukla, Fran, and Ollie.' Ostensibly a children's show, 'Kukla, Fran and Ollie' began on WBKB in Chicago in 1947 and in the fall of 1948 moved to a nightly half-hour on NBC. The Kuklapolitan Players were a group of hand-puppets whose personalities – and sophisticated levels of wit and whimsy – were more suited to adult viewers, who, in fact, watched the program in great numbers.

The two main characters were Kukla, the young 'human' puppet, and Oliver J Dragon (who resembled, respectively and by coincidence, the docile Pogo and blustery Albert of the *Pogo* comic strip that made its national debut in newspapers in 1949). Other puppets included Fletcher Rabbit, Colonel Crackie, Delores Dragon, Beulah Witch, Cecil Bill,

Birdley, Webley Webster, O Leo Lahey, and producer T Wilson Messy ('This has been a Messy production'). Among the parodies Bob and Ray mounted were 'One Fella's Family' (based on radio's 'One Man's Family'); 'Mary Backstage, Noble Wife' (based on 'Mary Noble, Backstage Wife'); and 'Mr Trace, Keener Than Most Persons' (based on 'Mr Keene, Tracer of Lost Persons'). Their regularly scheduled shows went off the air in 1954, but they remained top entertainers.

'Mama' made its television debut in 1949 and became a Golden Age institution, running through 1956. Based on the Broadway play 'I Remember Mama' – which was, in turn, based on Kathryn Forbes's book 'Mama's Bank Account' – the program was a warm comedy-drama that was both a domestic piece and period piece. Starring Peggy Wood in the title role, 'Mama' concerned a family of Norwegian immigrants in 1910 San Francisco. Each episode was introduced and seen through the eyes of Katrin, the eldest daughter of the Hanson household.

PREVIOUS SPREAD: *The immortal Honeymooners*

OPPOSITE: *Puppeteer Burr Tillstrom and his classic Kukla of the whimsical Kukla, Fran and Ollie.*

LEFT: *The hilarious Bob and Ray were as funny on television as on their major medium of radio.*

BELOW: *Matriarchal Peggy Wood as Mama . . . remember?*

Mercedes Rabbit and Madam Oglepuss. Fantasy, whimsy, satire and even parody abounded, with a lot of in-jokes and off-stage laughter by crew members.

In 1952 Kukla, Fran and Ollie shared their nightly half-hour with another set of players whose intellectual brand of zaniness also formed one of Golden-Age television's brightest moments. Bob and Ray made their television debut after serving as a comedy team on Boston radio. Bob Elliott and Ray Goulding fashioned their routines from the interplay of their off-beat personalities and their many alter egos, their main stocks-in-trade being satire and parody. Bob and Ray did takeoffs on radio serials, television programs (including news and weather reports) and commercials.

Among the real-life regular players on the 'Bob and Ray Show' were Audrey Meadows (before 'The Honeymooners'), Cloris Leachman (years before 'Mary Tyler Moore' and an Oscar in movies) and Durwood Kirby (before 'Garry Moore'). But among the memorable characters created by Bob and Ray and populating their inspired skits were: Linda Lovely, Wally Ballou, Kent Lyle

Each episode began with Katrin's narration: 'I remember the big white house on Elm Street, and my little sister Dagmar, and my big brother Nels, and Papa. But most of all, I remember Mama.' Katrin was played by Rosemary Rice, Dagmar by Robin Morgan, Papa by Judson Laire and Nels by a young Dick Van Patten.

It is interesting to note that two of television's earliest successful comedies were warm family series and matriarchal in structure. Here the similarities end, because the other comedy hit of 1949 began each episode with the mother sticking her head through a window and calling, 'Yoo hoo! Mrs Bloom!' 'The Goldbergs' had been a radio hit, created and guided by Gertrude Berg, and made an easy and successful transition to television.

'The Goldbergs' also dealt with family relationships and Jewish immigrant adjustments to be made in society. Berg herself tightly controlled the creative details – writing many episodes herself – and produced a series of remarkable integration and quality that introduced the ways of *yentas* to heartland America. Also in the cast were Philip Loeb as Jake (until revelations about Communist affiliations drove him from the cast, at which time he was replaced by Robert H Harris); Larry Robinson and later Tom Taylor as Sammy; Arlene McQuade as Rosalie; and Eli Mintz as Uncle David.

A family show more in the mold of the emerging television sitcom formula – de-emphasising familial relationships and stressing 'situations' and predicaments – made its debut in 1950. 'The George Burns and Gracie Allen Show' was just one more world to conquer for the legendary vaudeville, movie, and radio stars Burns and Allen. The premise was utterly simple: George Burns was in show business – providing opportunities for gags about their work and walk-on appearances by staff members – and was the calm center of the storms created by wacky neighbors, nutty friends and, especially, his zany wife Gracie. Through the years George Burns had been seldom more than a glorified straight-man for the harebrained Gracie Allen as she skewered common sense and chatted about her bizarre relatives. But television finally brought Burns into his own. He established eye contact with viewers and regularly spoke to them during the show; the device was taken to surreal heights during the final years of the program, when Burns installed a television set in his office that allowed him to view the mayhem being caused by his wife in the neighborhood (although, curiously, :+ never forestalled her predicaments).

TOP: *The Goldberg's dining room – complete with overhead microphone.*

RIGHT: *'Yoo hoo! Mrs Bloom!' Gertrude Berg as Molly Goldberg.*

ABOVE: *The Goldberg's dining room again (it was a center of the family's activities) with guest star Arthur Godfrey.*

Inspired writing – of both lines and situations – complemented the comic performances, making 'Burns and Allen' a classic of the Golden Age. Also in the cast were Harry Von Zell (playing, as he was in real life, an announcer), Ronny Burns (George and Gracie's real-life son), and, as neighbor Blanche Morton, Bea Benadaret. Blanche's husband Harry, the stuffy accountant, was played through the years by Hal March (who acted in several sitcoms and television musicals before hosting 'The $64,000 Question'), Bob Sweeney (a fine comic actor who eventually turned to television producing and directing), Fred Clark and Larry Keating. 'Burns and Allen' continued until Gracie retired in 1958; then George acted one season in a revised format that suffered without Gracie's non sequiturs. He later starred for a season with Connie Stevens in 'Wendy and Me,' and finally changed his persona into that of a monologuing roué with great success.

LEFT: *George Burns and Gracie Allen.*

ABOVE: *George and Gracie were among several show-business veterans who made transitions from vaudeville to stage to movies to radio to television. Previously Burns played the grumpy, harried straight-man to his wife's inane patter, but their television show allowed him to mellow and assume a deeper comic personality of his own.*

OPPOSITE TOP *Gracie Allen with Bea Benadaret, who played her neighbor Blanche Morton. Benadaret later played the mother Kate in Petticoat Junction, and provided the voice of Betty Rubble on the animated Flintstones.*

OPPOSITE, BOTTOM: *George and Gracie were joined in the cast by their real-life son Ronnie (left) in later episodes of The George Burns and Gracie Allen Show.*

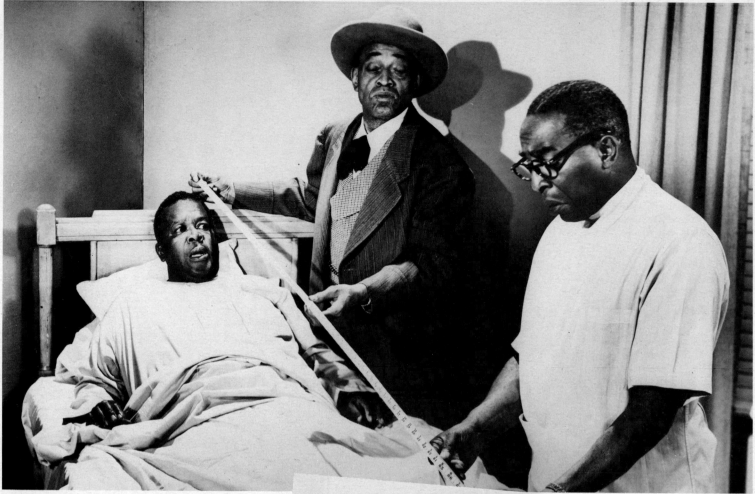

Another radio hit made a transition to television in 1951, but first it had some technical obstacles to overcome. 'Amos 'n' Andy' had been radio's biggest hit, but its creators and stars, Freeman Gosden and Charles Correll, were whites who portrayed blacks. So the casting call went out in order to mount a production in this new visual medium... and one of the finest ensemble comedy casts of any color was assembled. Alvin Childress played Amos Jones, level-headed cab driver and modest ballast of the cast, and Spenser William Jr played Andy Brown, oafish suitor of countless girl friends and gullible foil of scams. The centerpiece of the show, however, was George 'Kingfish' Stevens, played to great comic effect by Tim Moore. As head of the Mystic Knights of the Sea, a bankrupt lodge, he perpetually conned Andy into joining schemes and attempted to evade the wrath of his domineering wife, Sapphire.

These were situations of the most confounding order, and exaggerated performances resulted in a memorable classic. Protests, however, from civil-rights groups led to the series' cancellation, and, in 1966, to its withdrawal from syndication. 'Amos 'n' Andy,' which lasted for two years on television and featured the medium's first all-black cast, presented caricatured portrayals that offended many blacks. Other cast members included Ernestine Wade as Sapphire; Horace Stewart as Lightnin', the janitor; Lillian Randolph as Madame Queen, one of Andy's former girl friends; and Johnnie Lee as conniving lawyer Algonquin J Calhoun.

Another show featuring a black star was a major part of Golden Age television, although the premise of Beulah – about a black maid serving a white suburban family – probably didn't elate many civil-rights activists. Millions of viewers, however, (many of them, presumably, black) enjoyed 'Beulah' as she dispensed wisdom to the Henderson family and to her friend Oriole (played by Butterfly McQueen) on their predicaments. During Beulah's three years (1950-53), the domestic was played by Ethel Waters, Hattie McDaniel and Louise Beavers.

The last great superstar of radio to make the transition to television was Jack Benny, who proceeded cautiously, in an almost stingy manner, befitting his carefully cultivated persona. Beginning in 1950 Benny hosted periodic variety reviews featuring comedy and stellar guest lists. In 1952 he finally inaugurated his own half-hour comedy program – and one of the golden moments of the Golden Age. 'The Jack Benny Program' was not really a situation comedy except as it dealt loosely with the domestic and professional tribulations of the star (in the first few years, before her retirement, Benny's wife Mary Livingstone played herself on the show). Otherwise the series was a comedy variety program of skits, monologues and music, the foremost example of a series built on the personality of the star.

Part of Benny's persona was the humiliation and insults he allowed himself to suffer at the hands of second bananas. Together with his dozens of running schticks – being forever 39, keeping his hard-earned pennies in an impenetrable vault, his noisy Maxwell auto, his vanity about blue eyes and his prowess on the violin – enabled a brilliant ensemble cast of supporting players to combine for the comfort of predictability and the freshness of variations. Among the cast were Dennis Day, the daffy Irish tenor; Eddie 'Rochester' Anderson, Benny's sarcastic valet; the headstrong announcer Don Wilson (and his pampered son, likewise overweight, named Harlow); the impertinent store clerk Frank Nelson ('Yesssss?'), who surrealistically worked behind every store counter where Benny would shop; and the Man of a Thousand Voices, Mel Blanc. Blanc (who gave life to the Warner Brothers' stable of animated characters like Bugs

OPPOSITE, TOP: A classic, not only of Golden Age television, but of American comedy, was Amos 'n' Andy. Here the Kingfish (Tim Moore, center) and lawyer Algonquin J Calhoun (Johnnie Lee) measure the suspicious Andy (Spencer Williams). Pressure from civil-rights groups forced Amos 'n' Andy off the air.

OPPOSITE, BOTTOM: Another casualty of pressure groups was the warm comedy Beulah (here portrayed by Louise Beavers, with Ruby Dandridge on her shoulder).

TOP: Jack Benny with two of his most famous supporting players: Eddie 'Rochester' Anderson, and the fabled, noisy, run-down Maxwell auto.

ABOVE: Benny would go to any lengths just to be able to play his violin – which, in real life, he did rather capably.

LEFT: Jack Benny regarded television warily at first, hosting several specials before inaugurating his long-running series.

FOLLOWING SPREAD: Jack Benny, the original comedian who got no respect, ultimately became the Golden Age's supreme comic.

Bunny, Daffy Duck and Elmer Fudd) played several running characters on the Benny program, including Professor LeBlanc, the weeping violin teacher who despaired of ever teaching Benny to play even adequately. He also occasionally played a monosyllabic Mexican, engaged in the predictable exchange with Benny: 'What's your name?' 'Sy.' 'Sy?' 'Si.' 'And your sister?' 'Sue.' 'What does she do?' 'Sew.' 'Sew?' 'Si.' Blanc was even the off-screen source of inspired sound effects like the chugging, dilapidated Maxwell, and the creaking vault door.

More than other comedians who made the switch from stage, movies and radio to television, Jack Benny had found his perfect medium. Just as his character evolved from one of somewhat arrogant egotism to that of being eternally set-upon, so too did television provide the perfect frame for his style. Benny's classic pauses and comic timing were funny enough on radio (one famous routine had a robber approaching him demanding 'Your money or your life!' followed by a minute of silence and finally Benny's 'I'm thinking! I'm thinking!'). But on television these devices were supplemented by eye contact and droll mannerisms. No comedian crafted so finely such a large assortment of inflections and routines central to his character, and so perfectly suited to the intimate small screen. Jack Benny was the finest television comedian of the Golden Age or of any period since.

In 1951 a red-haired comedienne kicked off probably the most familiar of Golden Age television series, the most situation-laced of all sitcoms, and probably the most often rerun of any in television. *I Love Lucy* starred Lucille Ball and Desi Arnaz, and was a legitimate television original. Lucy had been a Goldwyn Girl and was a veteran of several movies (she played a straight role in the Marx Brothers' *Room Service*); Desi Arnaz was one of a plethora of second-string bandleaders (his specialty music, like his own background, was Cuban). The husband-and-wife team had even made movies together, with moderate success, and had their own radio comedy show, 'My Favorite Husband,' upon which 'I Love Lucy' was loosely based. But these inauspicious origins, coupled with an unorthodox production arrangement that allowed the comedy team ownership of the series and performances filmed before live audiences, all combined to fashion a classic whose appeal has diminished little through the years. (In some cities 'I Love Lucy' re-runs are still shown four or five times a day.)

Of course the central appeal is the character of Lucy herself. She was physical at a time when television relied on visual antics to impress viewers. She was loud at a time when subtleties were lost over the unsophisticated airwaves. Her character was a magnet that attracted situations and predicaments, forever identifying her with the sitcom genre. But as her subsequent success in other 'Lucy' shows through the years has proven, she was more than the right comedienne at the right time in the right place. Her appeal has been universal, and her comedic talents, as well as her instincts, flawless. As Lucy would scheme and plan – always to meet with disaster – both her dreams and defeats revealed a childlike, if not childish, nature that has been the basic appeal of many great comedy stars – Chaplin, Laurel and Hardy, Harry Langdon and Lou Costello.

The theme of 'I Love Lucy' was as simple as that of 'Burns and Allen,' and not dissimilar. Ricky Ricardo, played by Arnaz, was in show business as a bandleader, and the episodes revolved around domestic and professional misadventures. Ricky's career was more central to episodes than Burns's, and many stories concerned Lucy's attempts to perform professionally despite Ricky's opposition. A small regular cast supported Lucy and Desi in their comic escapades. William Frawley and Vivian Vance played Fred and Ethel Mertz, landlords and friends in the Ricardos' New York apartment building. Images of Lucy doing outrageous slapstick turns are virtual icons of Golden Age sitcoms, but America's love affair with Lucy was deeper than quick laughs: when her son Desi Jr was born (he would be 'Little Ricky' on the program) it was a national event followed as closely as any news story. The black-and-white re-runs of *I Love Lucy*, if nothing else survives on high-tech television, will be a perpetual reminder, a flavor for future generations, of Golden Age sitcoms.

Lucy had many imitators. In 1952 two of them came along right on her heels, as it were. Joan Davis was dubbed (by her publicists) the 'Queen of Television Comedy' and starred in 'I Married Joan.' She played Joan Stevens, the wife of domestic-relations court Judge Bradley Stevens, played by character actor Jim Backus. Miss Davis could mug with the best of them, but her predicaments were eminently less believable than even Lucy's outrageous scrapes (one whole episode was built on the fact that she didn't have enough chicken to serve guests whom Brad announced he'd be bringing home). She did give Lucy a run for money in the slapstick sweepstakes; however, in one memorable episode of 'I Married Joan' she positioned herself

BELOW: *The woman who gave situation comedy its name was Lucille Ball, whose weekly predicaments convulsed millions of viewers and inspired a generation of imitators.*

BOTTOM: *It somehow seemed logical for Lucy to ride the subway in a quest to extract a loving-cup on her head.*

RIGHT: *The immortal cast of I Love Lucy: Desi Arnaz as Ricky; William Frawley and Vivian Vance as Fred and Ethel Mertz; and Lucy.*

OPPOSITE, BELOW: *Harpo Marx was among the many celebrity guests on Lucy through the Golden Age.*

inside an enormous institutional soup-pot to spy out the recipe for a chef's soup. As would be expected, she gained firsthand knowledge as the ingredients began to shower down on her. The fault with 'I Married Joan,' to put it mildly, was not in the stars, but in the writers, that they were underlings.

Gale Storm was another comedienne who cast herself in Lucy's mold. She starred in 'My Little Margie' as the rubber-faced, slapstick-prone daughter of widower Vern Albright, played by Charles Farrell. Farrell had been a Great Profile hero of the silent screen in real life, and after 'My Little Margie' served as mayor of Palm Springs, California. The premise of the sitcom was that Vern vainly tried to control his attractive and wilful daughter, while she constantly worked to transform him into a sedentary father figure instead of the flirting ladies' man he was. Each episode featured the stars' framed photos on a bureau, each coming to life and explaining to viewers that 'I've got a problem . . . believe me, I've got a problem' with the other. 'My Little Margie' ran from 1952 to 1955 and was syndicated for years thereafter. Oddly, the program was one of the few television shows that spawned a radio spinoff; it ran concurrent to the television show with the same actors but different scripts.

Later in the Golden Age – from 1956 to 1962 – Gale Storm starred in 'Oh, Susanna,' a sitcom wherein she played the frenetic and predicament-prone social director of the cruise ship SS *Ocean Queen*. As Susanna Pomeroy, her foils were Miss Nugent (Nugey, the ship's beauty-parlor matron, played by Zasu Pitts) and the blustery Captain Huxley (played by Roy Roberts).

The comedy year 1952 produced a television hit that traveled the traditional radio-to-television route: 'Our Miss Brooks,' starring Eve Arden. The former screen star moved virtually the entire radio cast with her as she played the comely high-school teacher Constance Brooks. Gale Gordon, typecasting himself in preparation for later series and countless 'Lucy' shows, played the blustery principal, Osgood Conklin. Richard Crenna played the crack-voiced adolescent Walter Denton (years before more mature roles on 'The Real McCoys,' 'Slattery's People,' and 'It Takes Two'), and Robert Rockwell played Miss Brooks's romantic interest, the science teacher Mr Boynton. (In the last year of the series, 1957, Gene Barry played her new romantic interest.)

'Mr Peepers' proved that not all television comedy, even in the immediate wake of Lucille Ball, had to be madcap and slapstick. Peepers, played to fine form by Wally Cox, was also a schoolteacher, but the pace of this program was reserved and more whimsical. Peepers was what a later generation might call wimpy, but in his quiet manner he always managed to come out on top of situations: he even wound up marrying his equally shy, plain-Jane sweetheart in the show, Nancy Remington (played by Patricia Benoit). The scripts, as well as the performances, were very sensitive. Brash Harvey Weskitt was played by Tony Randall, and the delightful character actor Marion Lorne – a female Hugh Herbert if ever there was one – played Mrs Gurney; Ernest Truex played Nancy's father.

OPPOSITE, TOP: *Joan Davis, star of* I Married Joan, *was perhaps the most physical of the comediennes who followed Lucille Ball's cues.*

LEFT: *Gale Storm was Margie Albright and Charles Farrell her father Vern in* My Little Margie.

TOP RIGHT: *Eve Arden was Constance in* Our Miss Brooks, *and in the show's last season (1957) her romantic interest was provided by Gene Barry.*

RIGHT: *The tenderest moment of Wally Cox's Mr Peepers was the marriage of schoolteachers Peepers and Nancy Remington (Patricia Benoit).*

ABOVE: *The 1950s all American family, the Nelsons – David, Ricky, Harriet and Ozzie. Ozzie and Harriet helped propel Rick to a singing career, but not as a Hawaiian.*

One of the certified smashes, in its quiet way, of Golden Age television was 'Ozzie and Harriet.' A success for eight years as a radio comedy-serial, it made its debut on television in 1952 and ran through 1966. The Nelson family portrayed themselves – the credits dutifully listing the actors and their character names, which were identical – in this prototypical suburban series. Ozzie Nelson and his wife Harriet (in real life the former bandleader Ozzie Nelson and his lead singer Harriet Hillyard) were the parents of David and Ricky, prototypical American kids.

If Ricky Ricardo portrayed the soon-to-be-familiar television husband whose short periods of normality were interrupted by schemes of the daffy wife and necessary doses of patience on his part, then Ozzie Nelson typified the television husband-and-father of the aimless (but evidently fairly prosperous) and bumbling sort. He didn't pioneer this dubious character type – Stu Erwin (in 'The Trouble with Father') had done it in 1951 – but Ozzie became the stereotype for many similar shows and many critiques of the 1950s genre.

Ozzie never seemed to have a job, or at least to report to one, and Harriet was perpetually tidying up an already tidy household. Although David and Ricky were fairly typical, if bland, young boys, it was the father's scrapes, not theirs, around which the plots revolved. Don DeFore and Lyle Talbot were among the neighborhood friends of Ozzie who met at the golf club or at the hardware store. When the boys grew up, Ricky followed in his parent's footsteps and became a singer-musician himself. In fact, his records – coupled with the promotion they received when he performed his songs at the close of each show – transformed Ricky Nelson into a major rock 'n' roll star. At a time when Elvis Presley shocked the Establishment with his sexual gyrations, Ricky Nelson was pleasant, safe and as middle-American as the street in Hillsdale (state never identified) where the Nelsons lived. Incidentally, just as Ozzie's job was never referred to through the years, Ricky's singing was only germane to the shows' closing moments, when dozens of swooning teenage girls would somehow appear in the Nelsons' living room to hear him play and sing.

The program was actually titled 'The Adventures of Ozzie and Harriet.' A milder set of adventures could not be imagined, but their tenor was exactly what America seemed to enjoy voraciously for 19 seasons . . . and, since then, in re-runs. Whether Hillsdale was a comfortable reflection or a wistful daydream, viewers were intensely loyal to the family they grew up with, the Nelsons.

A different sort of family – a blue-collar clan of the type infrequently seen on television then or now – began its regular run on the second day of 1953. 'The Life of Riley' starred former motion-picture heavy William Bendix as the mildly tormented and befuddled Chester A Riley, a riveter at an aircraft plant. Sympathizing with, if not causing, his travails, were family members Peg (his wife, played by Marjorie Reynolds), daughter Babs (Lugene Saunders), son Junior (Wesley Morgan), neighbor Gillis (Tom D'Andrea), Honeybee Gillis (Gloria Blondell), and friends Waldo Binny (Sterling Holloway) and Otto Schmidlap (Henry Kulky). Martin Milner played Don Marshall, Babs's boyfriend. In a line that epitomized the mock-crises that formed the sitcom genre, Riley would look at the viewer at some point during each episode and exclaim, 'What a revoltin' development *this* turned out to be!'

This was actually the second incarnation of the character. In 1949, on the DuMont network, Jackie Gleason had starred as Riley (with Rosemary DeCamp as his wife and Gloria Winters and Lanny Rees as the children). Gleason was about to find greener pastures as comedy host of a variety program that would, in turn, spawn sitcom classics. His 'Life of Riley' is one of a handful of TV comedies that feature no audience laughs, whether real or 'canned,' and viewing the episodes – which display creditable writing and acting – make one realize how integral the 'laugh track' is to television comedy.

'Make Room for Daddy' was a Danny Thomas vehicle and still another series wherein the star portrayed a show-business personality. Thomas played Danny Williams, a nightclub singer whose work inevitably interfered with his family life. The situation arose from his performing activities and humorous family crises, all underpinned by character actors like Sid Melton (who played Danny's club manager) and Hans Conreid (who played Danny's Lebanese uncle, Tonoose). Between 1953 and 1964 there were two versions of the program, with minor cast changes made in 1957 when Thomas switched from ABC to CBS. Moreover, in the 1960s there were two television movies updating

RIGHT: *The rest of the Riley household: Marjorie Reynolds as wife Peg; Lugene Saunders and Wesley Morgan as kids Babs and Junior.*

BELOW: *'What a revoltin' development this turned out to be!' were the words William Bendix would utter over each week's situation in the sitcom* The Life of Riley.

BOTTOM: *The original Chester A Riley was Jackie Gleason, and his wife was portrayed by Rosemary DeCamp, who later appeared in* Love That Bob! *and* The Baileys of Balboa.

the growth of the Williams clan, and in 1970 a new program, 'Make Room for Granddaddy,' which ran for one season with many of the familiar cast members.

The Thomas program also served as a production wellspring for many other series. Its producer was Sheldon Leonard (former motion-picture heavy), who later produced such series as 'The Dick Van Dyke Show' and 'I Spy.' Mary Tyler Moore, who played Van Dyke's wife, later formed her own production company and launched her own legendary series, as well as 'Rhoda,' 'Hill Street Blues,' 'St Elsewhere,' and 'Remington Steele.' Bill Cosby, co-star of 'I Spy,' went on to many television successes, including 'Fat Albert' in animation and his own 'Cosby Show' smash of the 1980s. Danny Thomas's son Tony formed his own production company which would be responsible for 'The Practice' (starring Danny Thomas), 'Soap,' 'Benson,' and 'The Golden Girls.' In addition, an episode of 'Danny Thomas' featured the Williams family running afoul of rural Southern justice; the sheriff caught on with the public, and soon a spinoff series, 'The Andy Griffith

Show,' was a national hit and a special part of television comedy. Andy's adventures in Mayberry started when the Golden Age ended, in 1960, and spawned other spinoffs of their own, including 'Gomer Pyle'; they also provided the first series work for Ronny Howard, who later starred in 'Happy Days.'

Ann Sothern, a platinum movie queen (who was shot on television from the waist up, reportedly to obscure less regal proportions below), played Susie McNamara in 'Private Secretary.' Her only job requirement seemed to be getting her boss Peter Sands – Don Porter, later the television father of Gidget – out of embarrassing situations. His archrival in the business world was played by Jesse White, one of the Golden Age's most durable character actors. In 1957 the 'Ann Sothern Show' began, with the star performing similar turns as Katy O'Connor, assistant manager of the Bartley House Hotel. At first her boss was played by Ernest Truex, then, again, by Don Porter; among the supporting players were Jesse White (again), Louis Nye and Ken Berry.

Betty White has acted in many situa-

tion comedies through the years, but her first starring vehicle was 1953's 'Life with Elizabeth.' The trademark ending of each episode would see Betty and her husband Alvin (played by Del Moore) arguing with another couple; the camera would pull back to reveal them on a stage, and the announcer would interrupt to ask the actors to bid good-night to the audience ... after which they would continue their tiff. Jack Narz, later a game-show host and brother of Tom Kennedy, another game-show host, had a supporting role in the series, which ran on DuMont. 'A Date with the Angels' was a later series starring Betty White.

Television's first fantasy-sitcom was actually derived from a book and a movie 20 years old: *Topper*. The Thorne Smith classic (Cary Grant starred in the motion picture) came to television with Leo G Carroll as the befuddled banker whose new house was inhabited by the ghosts of the former owners, who had been killed in an avalanche. Only he could see them, which made for some hilarious situations indeed, especially as George and Marion Kirby – not to

LEFT: *Danny Thomas and his original television family in Make Room for Daddy.*

ABOVE: *Special effects, fine comic performances, and quality writing distinguished* Topper, *with Leo G Carroll, Anne Jeffries, and Robert Sterling.*

RIGHT: *Ann Sothern, as Private Secretary's Susie McNamara.*

mention their martini-drinking St Bernard dog – were prone to practical joking, and Topper himself was more devilish than the average bank executive. Other players included Anne Jeffries and Robert Sterling as the Kirbys (they were also married in real life); Lee Patrick as the air-headed Henrietta Topper (she had a straight role in the movie *The Maltese Falcon*); Thurston Hall as bank president Mr Schuyler, never able to fathom Topper's explanations of the paranormal activities that surrounded him; and Kathleen Freeman as the Toppers' benumbed maid, Katie.

ABOVE: *Paterfamilias Leon Ames with his television family in Clarence Day's* Life With Father, *which ran from 1953 to 1955.*

OPPOSITE: *Possibly the Golden Age's most genuine family was the focus of* Father Knows Best – *a sitcom without slapstick and with sentiment and sensitivity. In this Easter vignette Kathy ('Kitten') shares an Easter egg with her parents as Bud and Betty ('Princess') look on.*

Another classic book was called upon as inspiration for a television version in 1953. 'Life with Father' was based on Clarence Day's wonderful reminiscences, and Leon Ames played the blustery father who – even in this turn-of-the-century period piece – could not adjust to change in his world. 'It's a Great Life' was a short-lived but classic sitcom about two ex-servicemen in a boarding house teaming with the luckless brother of its owner, the trio perpetually but unsuccessfully conniving to reverse their financial straits. Michael O'Shea and William Bishop played the young men, with the Pat O'Brien-ish James Dunn as their elder partner; Frances Bavier, later Aunt Bea on 'Andy Griffith,' played the owner of the rooming house. 'Duffy's Tavern' – the radio classic – was the locale 'where the elite meet to eat' and starred Ed Gardner as Archie – 'Duffy ain't here' (he was never seen) – and Alan Reed, later the voice of Fred Flintstone, as Clifton Finnegan, neighborhood jerk.

Amid all the sitcoms that portrayed the American father as the suburban-neighborhood jerk, ineffectual, gullible and bland – and there would be many more such premises on television – one series particularly stood out as an exception. 'Father Knows Best' did not turn the tables on the genre (or the saying 'mother knows best') by making Mom the sap; everyone in the Anderson household was portrayed with respect. Everyone in the family – not just the father or the children, as in most sitcoms – could get into predicaments, but, most significantly, every member of the family could also help the others solve them. All had compassion and empathy, not in maudlin doses but mixed with some television silliness and a lot of realistic common sense. In short, 'Father Knows Best' made neither fools nor pontificating saints of its players, and the American viewing public took the program to its collective heart. It ran between 1954 and 1963.

'Father Knows Best' was originally a radio series, and star Robert Young (playing patriarch Jim Anderson) was the only cast member to make the transition to the tube. On television, Jane Wyatt played his wife Margaret; Elinor Donahue played daughter Betty; Billy Gray was the son, Bud; and Lauren Chapin played the youngster Kathy. The medium being television and the genre being the sitcom, there were many times when the characters *did* get into scrapes, and many of them were fatuous. But 'Father Knows Best' offered the public something most other sitcoms cared not – or dared not – indulge in: three-dimensionality. Characters were vulnerable and occasionally cried between the laughs. So did viewers, and that made 'Father Knows Best' a classic of the Golden Age.

Spring Byington was the first Golden Girl of the Golden Age. In 'December Bride,' she played Lily Ruskin, a widowed mother who lived with her daughter Ruth and her husband of eight years, Matt Henshaw (the couple was played by Frances Rafferty and Dean Miller). Adding interest were several colorful character actors, including Harry Morgan (playing Pete Porter) and Verna Felton (as Hilda Crocker); Morgan and Felton were to act in many series through the years. Morgan, in fact, spun off into his own series, 'Pete and Gladys,' with Cara Williams playing his wife, who had been frequently referred to but never seen in 'December Bride.'

Between 1954 and 1961, switching among all three major networks during its run, was 'Love That Bob,' featuring Bob Cummings, a moving-picture idol, and scores of gorgeous young models. Cummings played Bob Collins, a fashion photographer and ladies' man, so the show's built-in premise evidently was sufficient to attract several audiences simultaneously and to ensure its long run. Also in the cast were Rosemary DeCamp as Bob's widowed sister Margaret, and her son – a junior man-about-town emulating his uncle – Chuck, played by Dwayne Hickman. Supporting roles were played by familiar character actors Ann B Davis (as Schultzy the secretary) and King Donovan (as Bob's friend Harvey Helm). Lyle Talbot, Nancy Culp, and Rose Marie also appeared in 'Love That Bob,' and Joi Lansing was chief among the bevy of beauties who populated Bob's studio.

Two comedies began in 1955 that were destined to become classics of the Golden Age, series that will live forever in history, appreciation and re-runs: 'The Honeymooners' and 'You'll Never Get Rich' (later known as 'Sgt Bilko' and 'The Phil Silvers Show').

'The Honeymooners' was actually not a new creation in 1955. Jackie Gleason had purchased the television rights to radio's classic comedy 'The Bickersons' (with Don Ameche and Frances Langford), which had featured a shrill, constantly arguing husband and wife as its preoccupation. On his DuMont comedy-variety program *Cavalcade of Stars* (1950), however, Gleason and his writers changed the concept – the 'honeymooners' were renamed, made a bit more sympathetic and three-dimensional, placed in a lower-middle-class flat in Brooklyn and given neighbors. Gleason, playing Ralph Kramden, was joined by Pert Kelton, of grating voice, as wife Alice.

When Gleason inaugurated 'The Jackie Gleason Show' on CBS in 1952 'The Honeymooners' were an occasional skit on his hour-long show. In 1955 the segment became its own program, a half-hour replacing the regular Gleason show. Inexplicably – in hindsight it seems hard to believe – the series failed to establish itself, and in 1956 the hour variety program returned, again with 'The Honeymooners' as a segment. The 1955 season, however, was recorded on a process developed by DuMont, the ElectroniCam system of filming before a live audience. It is these 'Classic 39' episodes that have lived in syndication, although in 1985 Gleason resurrected many more segments from his variety show that did not happen to fit neatly into 30-minute formats; these were shown on cable.

In one of the finest creations of Golden Age television, Gleason and his ensemble perfectly captured the mixture of love, pretense, angst and futility that the 'Honeymooners' premise established, and they flawlessly performed character roles that might have been fashioned by Goethe. 'The Honeymooners' was an unapologetic slice of Brooklyn tenement life – it was set, by the way, in the neighborhood where Gleason grew up – featuring Kramden, a bus driver; his wife Alice, an unglamorous, houseworn partner; his buddy Ed Norton, a happy-go-lucky and gullible sewer worker; and Ed's wife Trixie, loyal helpmeet. Kramden and Norton were members of the Raccoon Lodge, and frequently engaged in schemes to alleviate their lowly financial states. A superb staff of comedy writers supplied serviceable premises and clever lines in the stories, and the performances were consistently inspired. Carney was the quintessential fall guy and Gleason's persona – blustery braggadocio inevitably giving way to humble contrition – fit into the childlike mold that traditionally served comedians so well.

'The Honeymooners,' however, con-

RIGHT: *The cast of* The Honeymooners: *Gleason as Kramden, Audrey Meadows as Alice, Art Carney and Joyce Randolph as Ed and Trixie Norton.*

OPPOSITE, BOTTOM: *The dingy apartment, the old icebox, the grand view of tenement walls – all were relieved by emotional spats and genuine tenderness in* The Honeymooners.

BELOW: *Jackie Gleason as Ralph Kramden. The pose was as famous as the line – 'One of these days, Alice! One of these days . . . Pow! Right in the kisser!'*

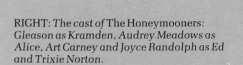

tained one more element that made for its immortality . . . an indefinable ingredient in its Gestalt. It is the quality that Gleason and his writers instinctively recognized 'The Bickersons' as lacking, and which is frequently referred to as 'chemistry.' Kramden could take advantage of Norton, but there was a boy-and-his-dog bond between them. The Kramdens could fight, but they always embraced at each episode's finis. Ralph threw up many fronts, but was utterly transparent. Warm sighs were as vital to 'The Honeymooners' as belly laughs, and viewers were very fortunate indeed to witness a magic convergence of quality writing and acting in Jackie Gleason's classic sitcom.

ABOVE: Phil Silvers was at home playing brash, fast-talking Sgt Bilko in one of the Golden Age's classic comedies, You'll Never Get Rich.

LEFT: Among the inspired crew of the Ft Baxter motor pool was Pvt Doberman (Maurice Gosfield) who could mug like no one else.

Phil Silvers played almost exclusively for the belly laugh, but 'Sgt Bilko's' premise and structure required little more. And by hitting a different target just as consistently, Silvers and creator-chief writer Nat Hiken forged another comedy classic. The setting is Fort Baxter, Kansas, an Army base presumably run by Col John Hall (played to great effect by Paul Ford, whose hangdog expression alone evoked laughs), but actually lorded over by the scheming money-hungry motor pool sergeant, Ernie Bilko. Silvers, a former burlesque comedian, was typecast beautifully and supported by a splendid ensemble of talented character actors. Harvey Lembeck and Allen Melvin were Bilko's henchmen, Corporals Barbella and Henshaw, and the hapless group of motor-pool privates were played by Maurice Gosfield (Doberman), Billy Sands (Paparelli), Herbie Faye (Fender), and Mickey Freeman (Zimmerman). Mess Sgt Rupert Ritzik was played comically by Joe E Ross, and Beatrice Pons played his nagging wife. Bit parts in the series were played by Fred Gwynne, Paul Lynde, Jack Healy, Elizabeth Frazer, George Kennedy and Charlotte Rae.

Every harebrained scheme in the world seemed logical when Bilko adopted it, often donning costumes and converting entire military buildings into gambling casinos. The high-decibel studio audience was poised like a mousetrap for every laugh, but the laughs were easy and frequent (one of Hiken's writers was Neil Simon, honing his skills for dozens of Broadway and Hollywood comedies). Sgt Bilko bilked everyone he met until the series' demise in 1959, but the scams are reprised every day via cult-favorite re-runs throughout the world, in grainy, tinny – but precious – reminders of how good Golden Age sitcoms could be.

'Leave It To Beaver' was another WASP-suburban-family gentle sitcom, wherein the father always wore cardigan sweaters and the mother tidied up an already neat and affluent home. It was indeed a genre, and many carbon copies were to come before the Golden Age ended. Nevertheless, 'Leave It To Beaver' was a cut above the average. Its closest counterpart was 'Father Knows Best,' which was, arguably, something of a female-oriented show (Betty, for instance, was brainy and independent, and had to deal with those traits, which were somewhat untypical of the 1950s' woman). 'Leave It To Beaver,' on the other hand, can be seen as a sustained treatment of male relationships – father and sons, brother-to-brother – and the challenge of accommodating to, rather than merely surviving, 1950s stereotypes. It was a very preachy show, with Ward Cleaver, the father, dispensing lectures to his sons. Usually they were hard to argue against – if you were a kid, yourself, viewing the program – and dealt with the consequences of one's actions. The situations, then, in 'Beaver' sitcoms, were themes universal to childhood rather than contrived, outrageous predicaments.

In the warm cast were Jerry Mathers as Theodore 'Beaver' Cleaver, Tony Dow as his older brother Wally, and Hugh Beamont and Barbara Billingsly as the parents. Also appearing were Ken Osmond as the all-time stereotyped snotty teenager Eddie Haskell; Frank Bank as Wally's friend Lumpy, and Richard Deacon as his father, Fred Rutherford; and Bert Mustin as Gus, the local fire chief. Mathers and Dow left the acting profession after 'Beaver' but were lured back for stage performances together and, finally, in the mid-1980s, as stars of the reunion *Still the Beaver* (a television movie and, later, on Disney and Turner cable systems, a full-fledged series again). Hugh Beaumont had died, Wally became a lawyer and Beaver's

ABOVE: *Jerry Mathers and Tony Dow as Beaver and Wally in* Leave it to Beaver, *another Golden Age family sitcom, but one that was able to capture the perspectives of boyhood. The series was revived in the 1980s.*

wife had left him; the new version was indeed a 1980s update of the somewhat blander '50s, but the new 'Beaver' movie featured flashbacks of Ward's bedside lectures – black-and-white clips from the original series – as appropriate, and irrefutable, as always.

'The Real McCoys' was a family show with a twist. The sitcom's family was unlike the usual TV family: Amos McCoy was a widower who headed the clan of his grandson and his wife, who in turn were raising younger siblings not their own. 'The Real McCoys' also began a new category of sitcoms: creator and producer Paul Henning was to specialize in rural-oriented series about transplanted lifestyles. Later successes in his stable of shows included 'The Beverly Hillbillies,' 'Petticoat Junction' and 'Green Acres.' Walter Brennan, veteran character actor and three-time Oscar winner, played the crackerbarrel patriarch of the McCoy clan, and Richard Crenna played grandson Luke; Kathleen Nolan played his wife Kate. The children, Little Luke and Hassie,

were played by Michael Winkleman and Lydia Reed, and Tony Martinez played farmhand Pepino ('Si, senor Grandpa!'). Among the many supporting players was Andy Clyde (as George MacMichael), who had been a featured comedian with the Mack Sennett studio in silent days and was paired with W C Fields in several motion pictures of the 1920s.

More conventional family sitcoms rolled before the Golden Age faded. 'Bachelor Father' began in 1957 with John Forsythe as Bentley Gregg, prosperous and suave attorney, and Noreen Corcoran as his niece and ward, Kelly. The valet Peter Tong was plyed by Samee Tong. 'The Donna Reed Show' resembled many other family sitcoms, but could boast *two* teenage recording stars in its cast: Shelley Fabares (who played daughter Mary, and had a hit record with 'Johnny Angel') and Paul Peterson (son Jeff, whose real-life hit was 'My Dad'). The parents were Carl Betz as Dr Alex Stone and Donna Reed as Donna Stone. She had won an Oscar for portraying a prostitute in *From Here to Eternity*, but was definitely not typecast; 'The Donna Reed Show' was perhaps the most wholesome of all the family sitcoms. Bob Crane and Ann McCrea played the Stones' neighbors in the show, and in the last years of the series (it ran from 1958 to 1966), Patty Peterson played Trisha, a girl adopted by the Stones. 'Dennis the Menace' was one of several family sitcoms based on comics or cartoons ('Blondie' also was, twice, and 'Hazel,' starring Shirley Booth, was another). The TV Dennis was tamer than his comic-strip incarnation, more pesky than menacing and a bit cuter, as the series dealt with the situations caused by his inevitable misunderstanding of events. Jay North played Dennis, and parents Henry and Alice Mitchell were portrayed by Herbert Anderson and Gloria Henry.

Joseph Karnes played the irascible neighbor Mr Wilson (whose conflicts with Dennis formed the core of the show) until he died and was succeeded by 'Cousin' Gale Gordon, television's resident blustery neighbor; the two Mrs Wilsons were Sylvia Field and Sara Seeger.

The era of Golden Age sitcoms closed out with a program that, on the face of it, broke the mold of the 1950s stereotypes. 'The Many Loves of Dobie Gillis,' based on the book by Max Shulman, featured teenagers as main characters instead of supporting players in a family situation. It also broke tradition by letting the ne'er-do-well kid escape his comeuppance. Dobie himself – instead of his father or another adult – was left to moralize in soliloquies before Rodin's statue *The Thinker*. And the sitcoms' first protest figure, the beatnik Maynard G Krebs, who spouted Greenwich Village-cum-Hollywood lingo, was a sympathetic character, one who presumably would have shocked the denizens of Hillside and its counterparts.

All the protest and beatnik stuff was television-mild, of course, but the series, which commenced in 1959, dealt in Shulman's wry manner with angst and the American Dream. Dobie, a teenager in high school, coped with both his father's expectations that he join the family grocery and the impossible materialistic demands made by his heart-throb dream, Thalia Menninger. Conflicts about career commitments and romantic pursuits were punctuated by the antics of the feckless bongo-tapping Maynard ('You rang, good buddy?'), who added nonsense and non sequiturs along with the medium's first anti-authoritarian note, mild as it was. Television comedy – and American society in general – was to be awash in iconoclasm, the rule rather than the comic exception, in another decade's time.

But neither 'The Many Loves of Dobie Gillis' nor Maynard G Krebs himself had any subversive purpose. The series was good comedy, underpinned by an outstanding cast of regulars and bit players.

Dobie was portrayed by Dwayne Hickman, and Maynard by Bob Denver, who was to wash up later in television history – sans goatee – on 'Gilligan's Island.' Thalia Menninger was played by Tuesday Weld, just one of the actors from the series who went on to greater fame. (Others were Warren Beatty, who played Dobie's arch-rival Milton Armitage; Ronny Howard, later to star in 'Happy Days'; Jack Albertson, later to star in 'Chico and the Man'; and Jo Anne Worley, who would be a 'Laugh-In' girl years later.) Frank Faylen and Florida Friebus played the eternally distraught parents of Dobie, and Shiela James was Zelda Gilroy, the tomboy who seemed to be the only female who chased him. Others in the cast included Steve Franken (Chatsworth Osborne Jr); William Schallert (Mr Pomfritt); Darryl Hickman, Dwayne's brother (Davey, Dobie's brother); Michael J Pollard (Maynard's cousin Duncan); and Doris Packer (the mother of Armitage and, when Beatty left the show, Osborne). As the show continued through the years, the players obviously outgrew the high-school environs; later episodes place Dobie and Maynard in the army and in college.

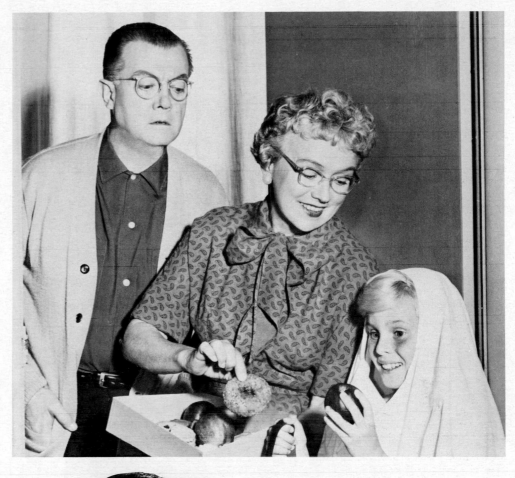

LEFT: *Donna Reed was a television mom who got herself in her share of scrapes. Paul Peterson, who played Jeff, is at her far left.*

ABOVE RIGHT: *Jay North, as Hank Ketcham's Dennis the Menace, in a rare moment of innocence, although Joseph Kearns (Mr Wilson) isn't so sure.*

RIGHT: *Bob Denver (later to play the lead in Gilligan's Island) as Maynard, and Dwayne Hickman (previously the nephew on Love That Bob!) as Dobie in The Many Loves of Dobie Gillis.*

Among the lesser successes and shorter runs in Golden Age sitcoms were 'Abbott and Costello,' who brought their routines to television via syndication; 'Ethel and Albert,' with Peg Lynch and Alan Bunce; 'Meet Corliss Archer,' with Lugene Saunders and, later, Ann Baker, in the title role; 'My Favorite Husband,' with Barry Nelson and Joan Caulfield; 'Easy Aces,' with Goodman and Jane Ace'; 'Meet Millie,' with Elena Verdugo and Florence Halop; and 'My Friend Irma,' with Marie Wilson.

J Carrol Naish switched ethnic types from Oriental (he had played Hollywood's Charlie Chan) to Italian as he starred in 'Life with Luigi'; Jack Lemmon and Cynthia Stone, at that time real-life marrieds, starred in 'Heaven for Betsy'; Eddie Mayehoff, Chester Conklin, Billie Burke and Arnold Stang star-

red in 'Doc Corkle.' Ezio Pinza tried his hand at sitcom work in 'Bonino'; Paul Hartman, Fay Wray and Natalie Wood starred in 'Pride of the Family'; Charlie Ruggles played the title role in 'The World of Mr Sweeney'; Peter Lawford starred in 'Dear Phoebe'; Willard Waterman starred in TV's version of radio's classic 'The Great Gildersleeve.'

Other sitcoms were 'Norby,' with David Wayne; 'The Aldrich Family,' another transported radio classic; 'The Ed Wynn Show,' wherein the vaudevillian played a kindly grandfather; 'Peck's Bad Girl,' with Patty McCormick as the tomboy; 'Leave It to Larry,' with Eddie Albert; 'Jamie,' played by Brandon deWilde; 'That's My Boy,' starring Eddie Mayehoff; 'Studs' Place,' starring Studs Terkel, later a famous writer; 'Joe and Mabel,' starring Larry Blyden;

'Where's Raymond?,' starring Ray Bolger; 'Halls of Ivy,' starring Ronald Colman and his wife, Benita Hume; 'The People's Choice' and 'Hennesey,' both starring Jackie Cooper; 'The Soldiers,' with Hal March and Tom D'Andrea; 'Love and Marriage,' starring William Demarest and Stubby Kaye; 'The Brothers,' starring Bob Sweeney and Gale Gordon; 'Stanley,' with Buddy Hackett and Carol Burnett; 'The Adventures of Hiram Holliday,' starring Wally Cox; 'Willy,' with June Havoc; 'Tugboat Annie,' with Minerva Urecal; and 'Fibber McGee and Molly,' another radio crossover, starring Bob Sweeney and his closet.

Anne Jeffries and Robert Sterling came back to life after being ghosts on 'Topper' in the series 'Dearest Enemy' and 'Love That Jill'; and the movie classic *How to Marry a Millionaire* was made into a sitcom starring Barbara Eden, Merry Anders and Lori Nelson. 'Too Young to Go Steady' starred Brigid Bazlen, and Dennis O'Keefe, and Hope Emerson starred in the 'Dennis O'Keefe Show.' Real-life Hollywood veterans and married couple, Howard Duff and Ida Lupino starred in the Hollywood spoof 'Mr Adams and Eve,' with Alan Reed as their producer. And although 'I Love Lucy' went off the air in 1956 (except, of course, for the omnipresent re-runs), 'The Lucy-Desi Comedy Hour' continued, with expanded adventures of the Ricardos, appearing as occasional features on the 'Desilu Playhouse' anthology series.

Nineteen-sixty is an appropriate year to mark the end of Golden Age comedy. Many 1950s-type shows continued to be introduced in the following decade, along with other fixtures of the Golden Age. But two types of show premiered in the 1960s, one of which was characterized by 'The Dick Van Dyke Show,' whose sophisticated writing marked a departure from the majority of Golden Age sitcoms. Others were a short decade away — but light years in terms of content and quality: the screaming, brash, vulgar sitcoms replete with insults, double-entendre and subjects that would have made Harriet Nelson and Donna Reed's characters blush even in private.

One of the canons of a nightclub comedian's survival is to reach down for the vulgar material when your audience slips from you. Golden Age television comedy was not always excellent, and it was often banal. But at its best it was unbeatable; later comedy series could conceivably reach as far, but never beyond. The shame of television comedy since the Golden Age is that it has attempted that reach so infrequently.

OPPOSITE: Bud Abbott and Lou Costello were hits on television when they added touches of surrealism to their considerable comedic routines. Sidney Field, Hillary Brooke and Joe Besser were supporting players.

LEFT: Gale Gordon (top) and Bob Sweeney played The Brothers in a short-lived (1956-1958) but funny and memorable sitcom. Sweeney later became a respected TV-comedy producer and director.

BELOW LEFT: Jackie Cooper – who had played Skippy in silent movie comedies – was Sock Miller in the low-keyed The People's Choice, supported by Patricia Breslin and Cleo, the thinking Bassett hound.

BELOW: The real-life husband-and-wife team of Ida Lupino and Howard Duff starred in the Hollywood-based sitcom Mr Adams and Eve between 1956 and 1958.

DRAMA
in the 1950s

If there is one area that compels the 'Golden Age' designation in television history, it is that of live drama. The source can hardly be nostalgia, since at least half of the viewing public today never saw the landmark productions of the 1950s. Also, live drama lays claim to special consideration because – quality aside – the other genres of the period, like situation comedies and even, occasionally, variety shows, are still with us. Live drama is not. It has been absent for many years, with its attendant creative accommodations and inherent devotion to excellence.

Television drama of the 1950s was indeed inherently different from television that followed. In the early days, television screens were small, and dramatic fare was obliged to rely on small casts, close-ups, few scene changes and relatively uncomplicated dialogue. Compromises with newborn technologies begot a very special form of dramatic presentation: television plays were intimate productions. Writers and producers had to forego the spectacular dimensions of the movie screen, and even shrink, in effect, the dimensions of the theatrical stage, heretofore drama's most intimate mode. Hence television dramas were those of personality rather than action; the focus was on characters, conflict and emotion. It can be argued that Golden Age television drama cannot be classified solely by the calendar and by the medium – a particular sort of play emerged, fashioned not only by television's limits, but by its potentialities.

During the Golden Age, live drama gave way to filmed anthology programs that carried on the same young traditions of live television for reasons that will be discussed below. In the beginning, the network system was very ten-

ABOVE: *Lillian Gish (center) in her television debut in* The Late Christopher Bean *(1949).*

tative, and New York was the center of the industry; the Broadway tradition, rather than the Hollywood flavor, influenced early television. Moreover, the film capital initially shunned television as a threat to movie theaters.

But in both live drama and the filmed-anthology dramatic series that closed out the Golden Age, a genre called 1950s Drama – introspective personality conflicts and tales intrinsic to television's singular demands – emerged.

A new crop of creators emerged too. Of course Golden Age television was replete with adaptations – everything from ancient Shakespeare to contemporary *Mary Poppins*, years before the movie version – but the real significance was in the original productions and the generation of writers, producers and directors who admirably answered the medium's call.

Among the impressive young writers

of the day were Rod Serling, Robert Alan Arthur, Calder Willingham, Horton Foote, Sumner Locke Elliott, David Shaw, J P Miller, Paddy Chayefsky, Gore Vidal, Tad Mosel and Reginald Rose. Directors included Sidney Lumet, George Roy Hill, Franklin Shaffner, John Frankenheimer, Delbert Mann, Arthur Penn and Robert Mulligan.

In the Fall of 1947, the Sunday nine-o'clock hour on NBC was given to a pair of anthology dramatic programs, the 'A.N.T.A. Playhouse' and 'The Theater Guild Television Theater.' The time slot was to become a virtual shrine for live television drama through the Golden Age. Before Dinah Shore made it her weekly home in 1957, the following Sunday-at-9 programs offered quality drama and comedy productions: 'The Philco Television Playhouse,' 'Masterpiece Playhouse,' 'The Goodyear/Philco Playhouse,' 'The Goodyear Television Playhouse' and 'The Alcoa Hour.'

Fred Coe was the producer and driving force through all the changing titles and sponsorships, and he displayed a fierce commitment to quality and originality. The most famous of 'Goodyear/Philco''s productions was 1953's 'Marty.' Paddy Chayefsky's play concerned a shy butcher and his awkward attempts at achieving some kind of social life. Rod Steiger sensitively portrayed Marty, and Nancy Marchand (later Mrs Pynchon on 'Lew Grant') played the homely girl who brought love to his life. The play was superbly directed by Delbert Mann, and later became a notable theatrical film – the first of several teleplays transferred to large-screen versions, a process that in itself testified to the quality emanating from the junior medium.

OPPOSITE: *Rod Steiger and Nancy Marchand in the Golden Age's classic live drama,* Marty.

LEFT: *In 1956 writer Paddy Chayefsky won an Oscar for his screen version of the teleplay* Marty; *he was congratulated by Claudette Colbert.*

Other memorable productions on 'Philco/Goodyear/Alcoa' included 'Ann Rutledge' (with Grace Kelly); 'Cyrano de Bergerac' (with José Ferrer); 'October Story' (with Leslie Neilsen and Julie Harris); 'Wish on the Moon' (with Eva Marie Saint); 'Old Tasselfoot' (with E G Marshall); 'The Expendable House' (with John Cassavetes); 'The Catered Affair' (with Thelma Ritter); 'The Man is Ten Feet Tall' (with Sidney Poitier); and 'Shadow of the Champ' (with Jack Warden and Lee Grant.)

In 1948 CBS introduced a drama anthology showcase that was to be another television landmark: 'Studio One.' Worthington Miner was the guiding spirit behind this series, and he, like Coe, had a commitment to fine acting and direction; he also brought an innovative sense of visual *élan* to his productions. Miner experimented with bold set direction and unorthodox camera angles, giving the small screen a sense of excitement, complementing the taut dramas and bright comedies.

LEFT: *Marsha Hunt in Shakespeare's Twelfth Night on Philco TV Playhouse.*

TOP: *Dennis King (right) as Ebenezer Scrooge in Dickens' Christmas Carol on Philco TV Playhouse.*

ABOVE: *Dorothy Gish followed her sister Lillian to the small screen when she starred (right) in The Story of Mary Surratt.*

ABOVE, FAR RIGHT: *Philco/Goodyear brought quality talent to television in productions like 1955's Cyrano de Bergerac with José Ferrer, Christopher Plummer and Claire Bloom.*

RIGHT: *Early Golden Age dramas — like 1948's Camille with Judith Evelyn — were simply televised stage productions, not yet using the dynamics of the small screen's own properties.*

Probably the most famous production of 'Studio One' was 'Twelve Angry Men' (another teleplay that was made into a theatrical-release movie). The high-pitched emotional drama, set in the jury room of a courthouse, was written by Reginald Rose and starred Robert Cummings, Franchot Tone, Norman Fell, and Edward Arnold. Other notable Rose teleplays included 'The Defenders' (with Ralph Bellamy, William Shatner and Steve McQueen), which became the basis for a series of the same name starring E G Marshall and Robert Reed; 'The Death and Life of Larry Benson'; 'Dino'; and 'Thunder on Sycamore Street.'

The very first drama offered on 'Studio One' featured two actors who were long associated with television. 'The Storm,' starring Margaret Sullavan, also included John Forsythe, who has been featured in 'Bachelor Father,' 'Charlie's Angels' (vocally, at least, as the unseen Charlie), and, most recently, 'Dynasty.' Dean Jagger also appeared, and he has been a familiar face through the years in series like 'Mr Novak' and as a guest (most recently on 'St Elsewhere').

In 1958 'Studio One' moved from New York to Hollywood . . . and died the same year. It was almost as if the symbolic transition from a theatrical to a motion-picture milieu doomed the integrity of live television drama. But during its run 'Studio One' presented an impressive array of dramatic offerings,

including 'The Scarlet Letter' (with Mary Sinclair); 'The Kill' (with Grace Kelly); 'Mary Poppins' (with Mary Wickes and E G Marshall); 'Mrs 'Arris Goes to Paris' (with Gracie Fields); 'Macbeth' (with Charlton Heston); and 'The Tongues of Angels' (with Leon Ames, Frances Farmer and James MacArthur).

OPPOSITE, TOP *and this page, LEFT: A landmark Studio One production was The Scarlet Letter by Nathaniel Hawthorne with Mary Sinclair as Hester Prynne and John Baragrey as Rev Dimmesdale.*

OPPOSITE, BOTTOM: *A young Charlton Heston starred with Lisa Kirk on Studio One in a modernized version of Taming of the Shrew.*

ABOVE: *Studio One's most memorable teleplay was* Twelve Angry Men, *starring, left to right, Norman Fell, John Beal, Lee Philips, Franchot Tone, Bart Burns, Robert Cummings, Paul Hartman, Walter Abel, Edward Arnold, Joseph Sweeney, George Voskovec and Will West.*

Mickey Rooney. Although the motion picture was a memorable production, it had only a fraction of the emotional impact of the 'Playhouse 90' presentation, which was truly one of television's finest moments.

There were many other first-rate dramas and comedies offered on 'Playhouse 90.' These included: 'Judgment at Nuremberg' (with Maximilian Schell, who reprised his role in the motion-picture version, Claude Rains, Melvyn Douglas and Paul Lukas); 'The Miracle Worker' (with Patty McCormick, Teresa Wright and Burl Ives, before the production went to Broadway and then Hollywood with Patty Duke); 'The Comedian' (with Mickey Rooney); 'Charlie's Aunt' (with Jeanette Mac-Donald and Art Carney); 'Face of the Hero' (with Jack Lemmon); 'The Last Clear Chance' (with Paul Muni); 'The Helen Morgan Story' (with Polly Bergen singing and starring); 'The Plot to Kill Stalin' (with Melvyn Douglas and Eli Wallach); 'Eloise' (based on the

humorous children's book and featuring seven-year-old Evelyn Rudie and a cast of mixed stars and celebrities including Ethel Barrymore, Charlie Ruggles, Monty Wooley, Louis Jourdan, Inger Stevens, Slapsie Maxie Rosenbloom and Conrad Hilton); 'The Edge of Innocence' (with Joseph Cotten and Maureen O'Sullivan); and 'Misalliance' (with Robert Taylor and Siobhan McKenna).

Other memorable 'Playhouse 90' performances included 'The Days of Wine and Roses' (with Cliff Robertson and Piper Laurie); 'The Velvet Alley' (Rod Serling's autobiographical drama starring Art Carney); 'Three Men on a Horse' (with Carol Channing and Johnny Carson in dramatic roles); 'The Time of Your Life' (with Jackie Gleason and Betsy Palmer); 'Eighty-Yard Run' (with Paul Newman and Joanne Woodward); and 'For Whom the Bell Tolls,' a two-part, three-hour presentation featuring Jason Robards, Jr, Maria Schell, Maureen Stapleton, Nehemiah Persoff and Eli Wallach.

ABOVE: *Jackie Gleason has proved as adept at drama as at comedy and music in his career. He turned in a memorable performance in 1958's* The Time of Your Life *on Playhouse 90. Co-starring was Dick York, later the husband on* Bewitched.

OPPOSITE: *The greatest moment of Golden Age television's finest form came with the live dramatic presentation of Rod Serling's* Requiem for a Heavyweight *on Playhouse 90 in 1956. This emotional tale of naiveté, cynicism, loyalty and betrayal starred Keenan Wynn (left) and Jack Palance; the drama also featured Ed Wynn.*

ABOVE LEFT: *Hallmark Hall of Fame brought famous names to television drama, and continues as a periodic series of specials. Alfred Lunt and Lynn Fontanne starred in Magnificent Yankee, about the life of Oliver Wendell Holmes.*

ABOVE: *Julie Harris played Joan of Arc in The Lark.*

OPPOSITE: *Hallmark brought Marc Connelly's legendary Green Pastures to television.*

LEFT: *Maurice Evans played Hamlet among other Shakespearean roles.*

'Hallmark Hall of Fame' made its debut in 1952 as a half-hour program; it later expanded its showtime and continues today as a series of periodic specials in the areas of drama and music. The program was inaugurated in 1953, and its first presentation was of Maurice Evans in 'Hamlet'; the play also featured Ruth Chatterton, Joseph Shildkraut and Sarah Churchill (who was the program's first hostess).

Other notable 'Hallmark' productions during the Golden Age included: 'The Green Pastures' (Marc Connelly's memorable black spiritual, starring William Warfield); 'Little Moon of Alban' (a powerful play about political tensions in Ireland, starring Christopher Plummer and Julie Harris); 'Macbeth' (with Maurice Evans, who was a producer-director with 'Hallmark' as well as star of its several Shakespearean productions, and Judith Anderson); 'The Little Foxes' (with Greer Garson, Eileen Heckart, Sidney Blackmer and E G Marshall; 'The Lark' (with Julie Harris as Joan of Arc, and Boris Karloff,

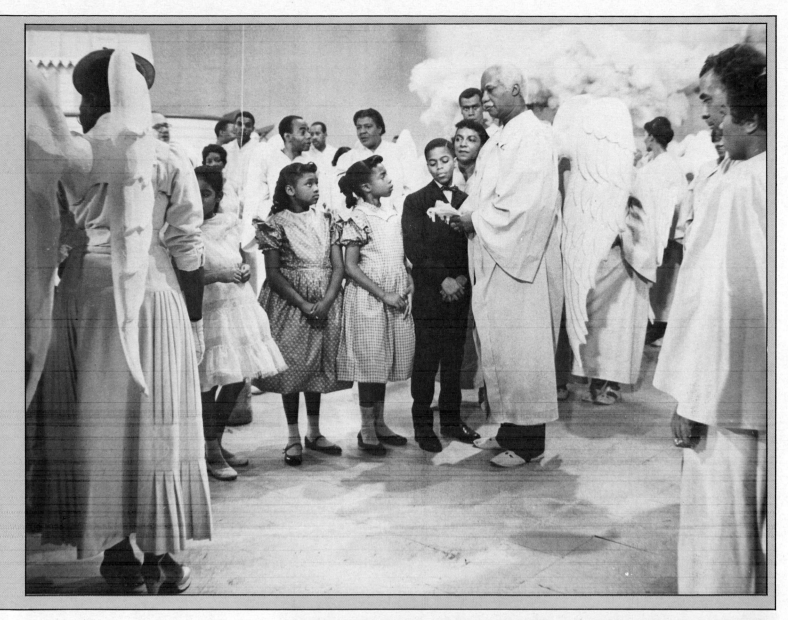

Basil Rathbone, Denholme Elliott, Eli Wallach and Jack Warden); 'Winterset' (with George C Scott, Piper Laurie and Charles Bickford); 'Born Yesterday' (with Mary Martin); 'Cradle Song' (with Judith Anderson, Anthony Franciosa, Susan Strasberg and Helen Hayes); and 'Man and Superman' (with Maurice Evans).

The 'Ford Star Jubilee' ran for just one season, in 1956, but managed to pack in many memorable dramatic productions, as well as the television debut of the classic *Wizard of Oz* movie. An impressive mounting of 'The Caine Mutiny Court-Martial' was perhaps its most memorable production; it starred Lloyd Nolan, Barry Sullivan and Frank Lovejoy. Other notable presentations were: 'This Happy Breed' (with Noel Coward and Edna Best); 'The Twentieth Century' (with Orson Welles and Betty Grable); and 'Blithe Spirit' (with Noel Coward and Lauren Bacall).

RIGHT: *Noel Coward headlined several productions of Ford Star Jubilee; here he is seen in a a production number with Mary Martin.*

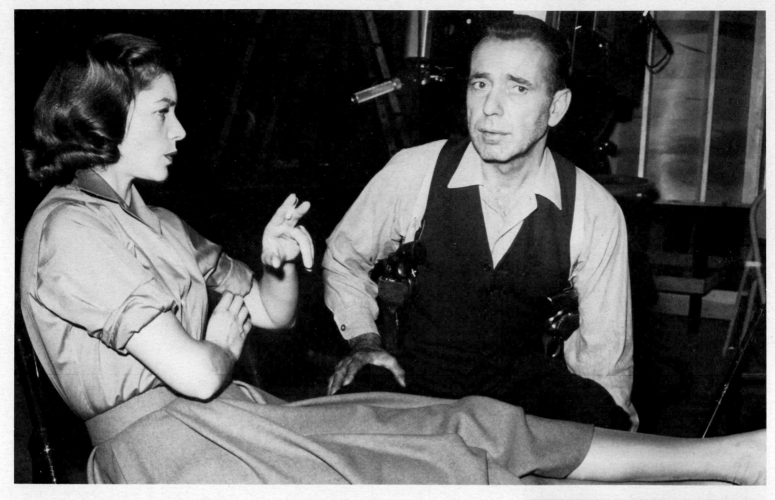

Fred Coe transferred his considerable skills to 'Producers' Showcase' in 1954; the program aired monthly and was 90 minutes in length, in contrast to his weekly hour on 'Goodyear/Philco.' The dramas (sometimes musicals and comedies) were more in the nature of spectaculars – a television-age word coined to connote a production of greater-than-usual scale. One of the most memorable dramas on 'Producers' Showcase' featured Humphrey Bogart's only appearance on live television in 'The Petrified Forest.' The teleplay, a version of Bogart's Broadway role of 20 years earlier, was directed by Delbert Mann and also featured Henry Fonda and Lauren Bacall.

Other landmark presentations on 'Producers' Showcase' included: 'Reunion in Vienna' (with Greer Garson and Peter Lorre); 'State of the Union' (with Joseph Cotten and Nina Foch); 'Mayerling' (with Audrey Hepburn and Mel Ferrer); 'Darkness at Noon' (with Lee J Cobb); 'The Great Sebastians' (the first pairing of Alfred Lunt and Lynn Fontanne on live television); 'Tonight at 8:30' (with Ginger Rogers and Estelle Winwood); 'Yellow Jack' (with Broderick Crawford, Wally Cox and Dennis O'Keefe); 'Dodsworth' (with Frederic March and Claire Trevor); 'The Barretts of Wimpole Street' (with Katharine Cornell); and 'Caesar and Cleopatra'

(with Claire Bloom, Sir Cedric Hardwicke, Judith Anderson, Cyril Ritchard and Patrick MacNee).

One of the most unique series in television history did not confine itself to live drama, although during its run, variously on the three major networks between 1952 and 1959, some landmark dramas were presented. 'Omnibus' was hosted by Alistair Cooke, American correspondent of the *Manchester Guardian* and the BBC, who, even after he became an American citizen, has continued to broadcast prescient and witty weekly 'Letters from America' on the BBC domestic service and world service. His pioneer television program was a cultural potpourri of live drama, interviews, music, education and even comedy. Broadcast on Sunday afternoons, and offering fare clearly more sophisticated and cultured than even the relatively higher standard of Golden Age television, 'Omnibus' evidently needed the support it received from the Ford Foundation to underpin its free-form approach. (Several imitations were spawned, however; they had even shorter lives and a lesser atmosphere of originality. One was NBC's 'Kaleidoscope' and another was producer John Houseman's 'Seven Lively Arts').

'Omnibus's most memorable production was actually filmed and shown

TOP: *Humphrey Bogart (seen here with wife and co-star Lauren Bacall) reprised his early stage role in his only live television drama* The Petrified Forest *on Producers' Showcase.*

ABOVE: *Katharine Cornell made her television debut on Producers' Showcase in* The Barretts of Wimpole Street.

OPPOSITE TOP: *Mary Martin first played Peter Pan on Producers' Showcase in 1956 and then reprised the role annually for several years.*

OPPOSITE BOTTOM: *Eddie Cantor in a rare dramatic role in* George Has a Birthday.

in biweekly episodes in 1953: 'Mr Lincoln' was written by James Agee and starred Royal Dano as the sixteenth president during his years of preparation. Other quality drama included 'A Lodging for the Night' (with Yul Brynner as François Villon); 'King Lear' (with Orson Welles); 'Oedipus the King' (with Christopher Plummer and William Shatner); 'The Virtuous Island' (with Hermione Gingold and Darren McGavin); 'She Stoops to Conquer' (with Michael Redgrave); and 'Mrs McThing' (with Helen Hayes).

If 'Omnibus' worked its wonders from the shaky branch of Sunday-afternoon programming, then 'Matinee Theater' was an even bolder experiment in a stranger time slot. For three seasons, beginning in 1955, producer Albert McCleery served a housewives' audience with five-day-a-week, hour-long live dramas. The demanding task resulted in a number of memorable productions including 'Wuthering Heights' (with Richard Boone, Natalie Horwich and Peggy Weber); 'Greybeards and Witches' (with Agnes Moorehead); and 'George Has a Birthday' (with Eddie Cantor in a dramatic role).

The 'Armstrong Circle Theatre' was broadcast for 13 years and represents perhaps the best example of a sponsoring company's commitment to image and excellence instead of ratings and a lowest-common-denominator approach that became a hallmark of television's later generations. Armstrong Cork Company's advertising agency – Batten, Barton, Durstine and Osborne – exercised a strong creative influence on the series and fought for quality through the persons of E Cameron Hawley and Max Banzhaf. Armstrong converted its honored radio drama anthology to television with such outstanding productions as 'The Man Who Refused to Die' (with Alexander Scourby); 'Have Jacket, Will Travel' (with Patty Duke); 'Ward Three, 4 PM to Midnight' (with Patricia Collinge); 'Assignment: Junkie's Alley' (with Addison Powell and Monica Lovett); and 'John Doe Number 154' (with John Napier). In its later years 'Armstrong Circle Theatre' concentrated on dramatic productions based on true-life incidents.

During the early years of television's Golden Age the movie studios were wary, to say the least, of their new sister medium. By the late 1950s most studios had finally gone into television production themselves, utilizing soundstages and personnel for television and theatrical movies quite compatibly. But when television was new, studios hesitated to rent their backlogue of films to broadcasters and actors were discouraged from appearing on television.

Robert Montgomery was the first major Hollywood star to enthusiastically enter the field of television, and he did it through the form of live drama. 'Robert Montgomery Presents' – occasionally entitled 'The Lucky Strike Theatre' – offered quality drama in a true anthology format, with Montgomery himself serving as host and sometime performer, as well as producer and narrator. Quality productions, many of them distinguished adaptations, were mounted, and – significantly – 'name' stars were persuaded to appear on the nascent small screen. Notable dramas included: 'Victoria Regina' (with Helen Hayes); 'After All These Years' (with Claudette Colbert); 'The Burtons' (with Kathleen and June Lockhart); 'Onions in the Stew' (with Constance Bennett); 'Sunset Boulevard' (with Mary Astor and Darren McGavin); 'Bella Fleace Gave a Party' (with Fay Bainter and J Pat O'Malley); 'The Lost Weekend' (with Montgomery as star); and 'The Great Gatsby' (with Montgomery, Phyllis Kirk and John Newland). Montgomery also assembled a repertory company of players (including his daughter Elizabeth, who would later star in the comedy series 'Bewitched' and several television dramatic movies) who would act in summer-stock type productions.

There were many other dramatic series, each mounting live productions with all the attendant logistical problems and demands, resulting, to be sure, in many routine plays. But in a symbolic reflection of the creative excitement generated by a brand-new medium of expression and communication, many masterpieces emerged as well. The Golden Age was still largely the period before networks took control of programming (and even time scheduling). Sponsors, ad agencies, and on-the-set producers had virtually free hands in choosing what to present, how to fill an hour, what portion of the viewing audience they intended to please . . . and with few more requirements than to create a quality production. Of course, it is easy to generalize about the creative freedoms of the Golden Age, just as it is easy to forget the inevitable portion of mediocre programs. However, it is hard to over-emphasize the difference between the creative ferment of the Golden Age and the dubious standards of most contemporary television.

Once the form and format of live television drama asserted itself, it quickly became a dominant part of each season's offerings; in 1950, for instance, a dozen live-drama anthology series were introduced.

Among the many other dramatic series of television's Golden Age — with some of their memorable productions — were: 'Plymouth Playhouse' ('Jamie' with Brandon DeWilde and 'Justice' with Paul Douglas and Lee Grant) and 'The Motorola TV Hour' ('The Brandenburg Gate' with Jack Palance).

'Camera Three' resembled 'Omnibus' — a cultural potpourri on Sunday *mornings* — but had a very low budget, which prompted such innovative compromises as stark set designs and unorthodox lighting mastered by producer/director Robert Herridge. Among the program's distinguished dramatic productions were 'Crime and Punishment' with Gerald Sarracini and 'Edgar Allen Poe: Israfel' with Geddeth Smith. 'DuPont Show of the Month' offered 'Harvey,' the brilliant pixilated comedy, starring Art Carney; 'The Fallen Idol' with Jack Hawkins and Jessica Tandy; 'The Prisoner of Zenda' with Christopher Plummer and Farley Granger; 'Windfall' (with Eddie Albert and Glynis Johns); 'Holdup' (with Hans Conried); 'The Winslow Boy' (with Frederic March); and 'The Shadowed Affair' (with Greer Garson, Douglas Fairbanks Jr and Lois Nettleton).

'ABC Album' presented television adaptations of prominent, contemporary fiction, such as 'Mr Glencannon Takes All' (with Robert Newton). 'Desilu Playhouse' presented a dramatic version of G-Man Elliott Ness's exploits, which later became a series vehicle for Robert Stack on 'The Untouchables.' 'Desilu' also offered 'Meeting at Apalachin' (with Cara Williams and Jack Warden); 'Dr Kate' (with Jane Wyman); 'Trial at Devil's Canyon' (with Lee J Cobb and Edward Platt); and 'Change of Heart' (with Robert Middleton and Dick Sargent).

'Douglas Fairbanks Jr Presents' was a half-hour drama anthology with the somewhat Hitchcockian theme of average people caught in unusual situations. Included in its five-year run were 'The Man Who Wouldn't Escape' (with Christopher Lee); and 'Second Wind' (with Michael Shepley and Nora Swinburne). Adolph Menjou, another screen personality, hosted 'My Favorite Story,' a series whose 'hook' was presenting dramas supposedly selected by guests. Prominent offerings during its 1952 season were: 'The Gold Bug' (with Neville Brand); 'Canterville Ghost' (with John Qualen); and 'Strange Valley' (with Kenneth Tobey).

OPPOSITE TOP *A Klieg's-eye view of the television soundstage during production of DuPont Show of the Month's Prisoner of Zenda.*

OPPOSITE BELOW: *A scene from The Auction, a presentation on Douglas Fairbanks Jr Presents, a series in which the host often starred.*

BELOW: *Most live drama series were sponsored by a corporation . . . such as Westinghouse (Studio One, Desilu Playhouse), whose spokeswoman was Betty Furness, later a 'consumer reporter.'*

'Ford Theatre' ran between 1950 and 1955, and presented dramatic productions of one-half and one hour in length, including 'A Touch of Spring' (with Irene Dunne and Gene Barry); 'Deception' (with Sylvia Sidney); and 'Sunday Morn' (with Brian Keith and Marilyn Maxwell). 'Front Row Center' was another anthology series, presenting such adaptations of famous fiction as 'Dark Victory' (with Margaret Field) and 'Tender Is the Night' (with James Daly, father of Tyne Daly of 'Cagney and Lacey' fame, and Mercedes McCambridge).

'Four Star Playhouse' was a unique drama anthology presented by the 'Four Star Studios' composed of four actors who frequently hosted and acted in the productions – Dick Powell, Rosalind Russell, Charles Boyer and Joel McCrea. The show began in 1952, but by 1955 Miss Russell and McCrea had been replaced by David Niven and Ida Lupino. The next year Miss Lupino departed to star in the comedy 'Mr Adams and Eve' with her husband, Howard Duff. A decade later Boyer and Niven teamed again, this time with Gig Young, on a wonderful ensemble series, 'The Rogues'. 'Four Star' offered quality drama, including 'Village in the City' (with Niven); 'Death Makes a Pair' (with Lloyd Corrigan and Jay Novello); 'The Collar' (with Niven); 'That Woman' (with Lupino); and 'Here Comes the Suit' (with Niven). The Four Star Studio went on to produce other television offerings as well.

'The Jane Wyman Theatre' offered another opportunity for a Hollywood star to host, and occasionally star in, various dramatic representations. Wyman's ex-husband, Ronald Reagan, would do the same thing in 'General Electric Theatre' and 'Death Valley Days.' Miss Wyman presented 'Helpmate' (with Imogene Coca); 'The Girl on the Drum' (with Jack Kelly); 'The Black Road' (with Robert Horton); and 'A Place on the Bay' (with Gene Barry).

'The Kaiser Aluminum Hour' presented powerful dramas like 'A Fragile Affair' (with Eli Wallach and Mary Cristoff); 'Man on a White Horse' (with James Barton and Barton MacLane); 'The Rag Jungle' (with Paul Newman); 'Antigone' (with Claude Rains); and 'Army Game' (with Paul Newman). 'The Pall Mall Showcase' focused on personal stress and conflict in half-hour dramas on ABC like 'Prisoners in Town' (with Carolyn Jones and John Ireland); 'Square Shootin'' (with John Newland); and 'Reunion at Steepler's Hill' (with John Ireland).

Continuing a list that can also serve as a roster of industrial corporations of the day, the 'Rheingold Beer Theatre' was hosted by Henry Fonda and offered such productions as 'Louise' (with Judith Anderson) and 'End of Flight' (with Edmond O'Brien). 'The Schlitz Beer Playhouse of Stars' was hosted by Irene Dunne and offered such dramas as 'For Better or Worse' (with Bette Davis); 'The Restless Gun' (a pilot for the series of the same name, starring John Payne); and 'The Unlighted Road' (with James Dean).

'Stage 7' productions included 'Appointment in Highbridge' (with Dan O'Herlihy); 'Debt of Honor' (with Edmond O'Brien); and 'The Deceiving Eye' (with Frank Lovejoy). 'Studio 57' on DuMont – one of struggling network's last programs – offered live drama in the form of 'The Haven Technique' (with Brian Keith) and 'The Engagement Ring' (with Hugh O'Brien). 'TV Sound Stage' was an early '50s anthology series that presented dramas like 'One Small Guy' (with Jack Lemmon) and 'Deception' (with Martin Brookes).

'The United States Steel Hour' was one of television's most enduring anthology dramatic series and provided some of its memorable moments of drama and comedy. Perhaps its most famous production was 'No Time for Sergeants,' a classic comedy starring Andy Griffith as country hick Will Stockdale drafted into the US Air Force. The teleplay was a combination of broad farce and dry personality situations, and became both a Broadway play and a feature movie, also starring Griffith. Other prominent productions of the 'US Steel Hour' were: 'The Bogey Man' (with Celeste Holm and Robert Preston); 'Freighter' (with Henry Hull and James Daly); 'Wish on the Moon' (with Eva Marie Saint); 'P.O.W.' (with Gary Merrill, Phyllis Kirk, Brian Keith and Richard Kiley); 'Incident in an Alley' (a Rod Serling play starring Farley Granger); 'Flint and Fire' (with Robert Culp and Gloria Vanderbilt); 'Mid-Summer' (with Jackie Cooper); 'Beaver Patrol' (with Walter Slezak); 'A Wind from the South' (with Julie Harris); 'The Girl in the Gold Bathtub' (a comedy with Johnny Carson); 'Funny Heart' (with Imogene Coca and Jack Klugman); 'Huck Finn' (with Basil Rathbone and Jack Carson); 'The Meanest Man in the World' (with Wally Cox, Betsy Palmer and Kenny Delmar); 'Bang the Drum Slowly' (with Paul Newman, George Peppard and Albert Salmi); 'Old Marshals Never Die' (with William Shatner); 'One Red Rose for Christmas' (with Helen Hayes and Patty Duke); and 'Family Happiness' (with Patty Duke and Gloria Vanderbilt). 'The US Steel Hour' was presented only every other week by the Theater Guild because of the elaborate productions.

For four years on CBS, and then for three years on NBC, with hosts like James Mason and Gordon MacRae, the 'Lux Video Theatre' offered many established Hollywood and Broadway stars their first television exposure. Among its productions were 'A Medal for Benny' (with J Carrol Naish); 'The Enchanted Cottage' (with Dan O'Herlihy); 'Miss Susie Slagle' (with Dorothy Gish); 'The Browning Version' (with Herbert Marshall); and 'No Sad Songs for Me' (with Wendell Corey and Viveca Lindfors). 'Lux Video Theatre' was one of several crossovers from a successful radio run.

Other dramatic anthology series of the Golden Age included: 'The Play of the Week,' 'Sunday Showcase,' 'The Buick Electra Playhouse,' 'The Revlon Mirror Theatre,' 'The Theatre Hour,' 'Sunday Showcase,' 'The Best of Broadway,' 'Cameo Theatre,' 'Actor's Studio,' 'Anywhere USA,' 'Medallion Theatre,' 'Suspense,' 'Danger,' 'Tales of Tomorrow,' 'Playwrights 56,' 'Color Spread,' 'Climax!,' 'Family Classics,' 'Theatre Time,' 'Bigelow Theatre,' 'Fireside Theatre,' 'Your Jewelry Showcase,'

'Cavalcade of America,' 'Star Stage,' 'O Henry Playhouse,' 'Damon Runyon Theatre,' '20th Century-Fox Hour' and 'Pulitzer Prize Playhouse,' which mounted productions of award-winning dramas. The 'Oldsmobile Music Theatre' experimented with a drama-and-music format (it was short-lived), and the syndicated '(   ) All-Star Theatre' allowed local stations to insert a local advertiser's name on the small-screen marquee.

Other memorable productions of 1950 TV drama, both independent offerings and presentations of anthology series, included: 'The Late Christopher Bean' (with Helen Hayes); 'A Day in Town' (with Charlton Heston); '50 Beautiful Girls' (with Grace Kelly); 'Flamingo' (with Steve Allen and Jayne Meadows); 'The House of Dust' (with Nina Foch and Anthony Quinn); 'The Day Lincoln Was Shot' (with Raymond Massey, Lillian Gish, Jack Lemmon and narration by Charles Laughton); 'The Man Who Came to Dinner' (with, naturally, Monty Woolley, Merle Oberon, Joan Bennett, Bert Lahr, Buster Keaton and ZaSu Pitts); 'The Bridge of San Luis Rey' (with Eva LeGallienne, Judith Anderson, Hume Cronyn, Theodore Bikel and Viveca Lindfors); 'Flight' (with Kim Stanley); 'Ah, Wilderness' (with Leon Ames); 'The Long Goodbye' (with Dick Powell as Philip Marlow); and 'I, Don Quixote' (with Lee J Cobb), the teleplay upon which the historic Broadway musical *Man of La Mancha* was based.

'The Devil and Daniel Webster' starred Edward G Robinson and David Wayne. Other Golden Age presentations included Ingrid Bergman's television debut in 'The Turn of the Screw'; 'The Wicked Scheme of Jebal Deeks' (with Alec Guiness); 'The Moon and Sixpence' (with Laurence Olivier, Judith Anderson, Hume Cronyn, Jessica Tandy and Geraldine Fitzgerald); 'Romeo and Juliet' (with John Neville and Claire Bloom); and 'Autocrat and Son' (with Sir Cedric Hardwicke, Christopher Plummer and Anne Francis). 'A Profile in Courage' starred James Whitmore as Sen Edmund G Ross of Kansas, whose single vote prevented the impeachment of President Andrew Johnson. The 1956 drama was based on a chapter from

ABOVE: *One of the memorable moments of original productions during the Golden Age was Andy Griffith's performance in US Steel Hour's* No Time for Sergeants.

LEFT: *Another landmark production on Golden Age television was Gian Carlo Menotti's opera* Amahl and the Night Visitors, *about a crippled boy cured for his act of generosity at the time of Christ's birth.*

his traveling the nation on the company's behalf, speaking to gatherings on the blessing of the free-enterprise system. Hence this television program had a direct effect on Reagan's interest in, and entry into, politics. Among the program's prominent dramatic offerings were 'The Windmill' (with James Stewart); 'Lady of the House' (with Myrna Loy); 'The Incredible Jewel Robbery' (with Harpo and Chico Marx); 'Flying Wife' (with Janet Gaynor); 'The Last Lesson' (with Charles Laughton); 'Clown' (with Henry Fonda and Dorothy Malone); 'The Stone' (with Tony Curtis); 'Mr Kensington's Finest Hour' (with Charles Laughton); 'A Turkey for the President' (with Ward Bond); 'The Girl with the Flaxen Hair' (with Ray Bolger); 'Man on a Bicycle' (with Fred Astaire); and 'The Half-Promised Land' (with Ezio Pinza and Mike Wallace, years before his performances in news programs).

'Death Valley Days' was also hosted for a time by Ronald Reagan and was, of course, an anthology of Western dramas (and some comedies). Among its productions were 'Kickapoo Run' (with Fess Parker); 'Lady of the Press' (with James Franciscus); 'The Lost Pegleg Mine' (with Andy Clyde); 'The Lady Was an MD' (with Yvonne DeCarlo); and 'A City Is Born' (with Reagan). Stanley Andrews ('The Old Ranger') preceded the future US president as host, and Robert Taylor and then Dale Robertson followed him in that role.

The television production technique of the *segue* was manifest in a programming sense as live drama gradually gave way to mostly half-hour, filmed anthology drama shows. Among them were 'Dick Powell's Zane Grey Theater'; 'Inner Sanctum'; 'The Loretta Young Show'; 'Shirley Temple's Storybook'; 'Confidential File'; 'Destiny'; and 'Panic.'

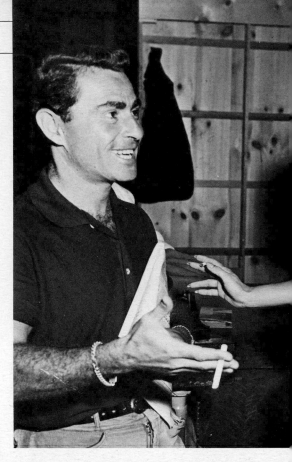

'Alfred Hitchcock Presents' was one of the most distinctive and durable of the filmed anthology series, the only continuing character being director Hitchcock with his macabre sense of humor. One feature of Hitchcock's dramas on television was their shattering of the industry code that forbade evil to triumph: he routinely announced in his closing remarks that the bad guys received justice, thereby circumventing the censors. However, he also ridiculed his sponsors and teased his viewers, so such disclaimers were taken seriously by very few. Among the outstanding presentations on the Hitchcock program were: 'Arthur' (with Laurance Harvey and Patrick McNee); 'Man From the South' (with Steve McQueen and Peter Lorre); 'Revenge' (with Ralph Meeker and Vera Miles); 'The Jar' (with Pat Buttram); 'Escape to Sonoita' (with Burt Reynolds); and 'Mrs Bixby and the Colonel's Coat' (with Audrey Meadows).

But for all the former movies stars and Hollywood directors who committed themselves to filmed anthology drama, none was more important – or made a more significant shift – than Rod Serling himself, the paragon of writer/producers of live television drama. 'The Twilight Zone' was his program, and, as with Hitchcock's bizarre themes and 'Zane Grey Theater''s Westerns, his offerings (a heavy proportion of them comedic) were preoccupied with science-fiction and fantasy. Serling's patented introduction set the mood each week:

'There is a fifth dimension beyond that which is known to man. It is a

dimension as vast as space and as time-less as infinity. It is the middle ground between light and shadow, between science and superstition and it lies somewhere between the pit of man's fears and the summit of his knowledge. It is an area which we call . . . the Twilight Zone.'

Among the teleplays, many written by Serling himself or Charles Beaumont, were: 'A Game of Pool' (with Jonathan Winters and Jack Klugman); 'Where Is Everybody?' (with Earl Holliman); 'The Silence' (with Franchot Tone); 'Night of the Meek' (a classic Christmas episode with Art Carney); 'A Stop at Willough-by' (with James Daly); 'Nick of Time' (with William Shatner); 'A Passage for Trumpet' (with Jack Klugman); 'The Hitchhiker' (with Inger Stevens); 'One for the Angels' (with Ed Wynn); 'The Tape Recorder' (with Keenan Wynn and Phyllis Kirk); and 'After Hours' (with Anne Francis).

'The Twilight Zone' was a consist-ently outstanding and innovative an-thology series, perhaps the most perfect mirror-image of the live drama in both its catholic range and its commitment to quality. It is no coincidence that Serling was responsible for some of the finest live drama as well as some of the best of that short-lived spate of filmed antho-logy that bridged the television gap to 'episodic' and 'action' dramas.

It is also significant that 'The Twilight Zone' made its debut in 1959, neatly – but somewhat gently – closing the decade and the fragile genre known as 1950s television anthologies, live and filmed, that helped so much to make the Golden Age golden.

CENTER TOP: *Rod Serling's activities neatly reflected the better aspects of Golden Age television drama. He wrote teleplays for many quality live productions, and hosted (as well as scripted) episodes of the classic Twilight Zone. He is seen here with guest stars Beverly Garland and Ross Martin from the episode* The Four of Us Are Dying.

OPPOSITE BOTTOM: *The master of the macabre – and of a singular sense of humor – was Alfred Hitchcock, who capably continued his successful movie directions while hosting a popular television anthology series.*

ABOVE: *Jonathan Winters and Jack Klugman in the first Twilight Zone episode,* A Game of Pool.

LEFT: *The title logo for The Twilight Zone.*

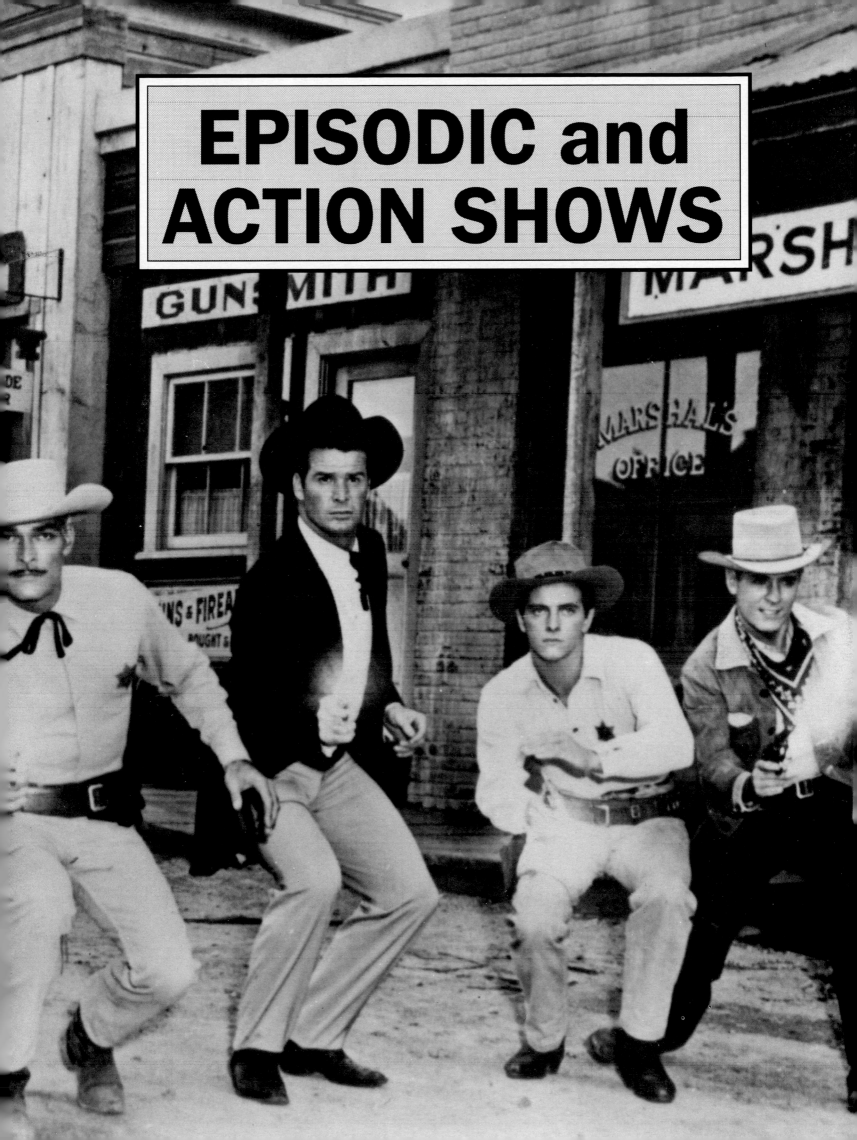

EPISODIC and ACTION SHOWS

A category of programs arose over the course of the Golden Age which we might call the episodic drama. Today it is a dominant form, and has virtually supplanted live drama. These filmed programs cannot truly be called mysteries, because their structure often reveals the perpetrators from the start; it is the chase, not the solution, that unfolds. Others cannot really be termed adventure shows, because they are series of chases at best; 'action programs' is more apt as a description. Many of them are only marginally dramatic, for they abound in light subplots, witty dialogue and humorous minor characters.

But 'episodic drama' is the best description of television's most utilized format after the situation comedy, and the adjective underlines the factor that killed the live drama as a staple of the medium. Episodic dramas featured a continuing cast of characters with whom the viewer could feel comfortable

— and want to watch every week. Viewer loyalty translated into ratings strength, and as the TV industry established itself through the Golden Age, advertisers and networks both came to surrender all other considerations to the ratings results.

The big breakthrough, however, in the switch from live to episodic drama was not in any aspect of the new medium's new technology, but in plain old film. It eventually dawned on studio and network executives that a live drama was finished for good after one performance and its attendant expenses. A filmed series, however, could be shown again at season's end, and a few years hence. It could be sold overseas and marketed to hundreds of local stations once the network decided it was finished with the cans of film. Actually, the surprising factor is that the networks didn't seize upon the device earlier.

In reality, one stumbling block was the inability to mount such productions. The logical facilities for large-scale film production were in Hollywood, and the old-line motion-picture studios were in a depression and could have used the activity and revenues. But television itself was one of the reasons for Hollywood's declining theatrical receipts, and the film community viewed television as the enemy. There are many reports of Hollywood's threats of blacklisting — not over Communist connections, but of actors who dared cross the line and work on television. Likewise, there are reports of Hollywood edicts that televisions could not be used as props in the homes of sympathetic actors on the screens. Eventually, of course, this relationship changed, and although it happened in a rather backward fashion, when it did the floodgates opened.

In the beginning, the studios were not chary of profiting from the fledgling

PREVIOUS SPREAD: *Warner Brothers's shooting stars from the Western series Colt .45, Cheyenne, Lawman, Maverick, and Sugarfoot.*

OPPOSITE TOP: *Roy Rogers and Dale Evans.*

OPPOSITE BOTTOM: *Hopalong Cassidy, one of the few good guys in a black hat.*

ABOVE: *George Reeves as the Man of Steel.*

medium. Warehouse prints of old movies were rented to stations plentifully (Jackie Gleason used to parody the schedules of late-night television by refering to 'The Late-Late-Late-Late-Late Show' and the movies shown thereon). But a Supreme Court ruling of the late 1940s was responsible for a crack in the door: the anti-trust finding ordered studios to divest themselves of theater ownership. United Paramount Theaters suffered financially because of the ruling, and opted to merge with ABC, the weak sister of the three networks.

With Paramount money, ABC turned around and invested in an oddball project from a Hollywood studio in return for their agreement to supply, and produce, material for television. The studio was Walt Disney Productions; their scheme was the much-ridiculed Disneyland project; and at the start the Mouse Factory actually viewed its weekly television hour on ABC as little more than an extended commercial – a chance to promote their theatrical movies, as well as Disneyland. The rest, as they say, is history. Disneyland became a phenomenal success, and ABC was salvaged. Paramount (the film production branch) learned that co-operation with television was not poisonous. Most importantly, everyone learned – as the Wednesday Evening 'Disneyland' top-ten ratings success proved – that motion-picture companies could use their existing facilities to make money in one more way.

The anti-trust ruling allowing studios to keep production and distribution operations but not physical ownership of theaters was practically an invitation to enter television production. It simply took Hollywood five years to realize it.

Another studio in financial trouble was Warner Bros. When Warners had been nearly bankrupt in the 1920s, it was the departure into sound movies that had saved them, and in the 1950s it was a venture into television. That move salvaged the studio and revolutionized the nature of drama on television. But whereas Disney and Warners pioneered the motion-picture marriage with television, they did not introduce the utilization of film.

There is a stereotype that all of Golden Age television was live – ensuring its wonderful spontaneity and representing its primitive individualism. In fact, a lot of early television was on film, even a few 'live dramas.' It just happened that

film was almost universally regarded as anathema in the young television community. Producers and actors saw television as closer to stage than film (in the beginning of the Golden Age, New York, not Hollywood, was the center of production), and it was felt that if film-studio methods were to be used, the crew might as well be making movies instead of television plays. As a new medium asserts itself, it naturally needs to define its parameters and establish a measure of independence.

So the early years of the Golden Age were a mixed bag of live productions and film. 'Action in the Afternoon' was a daily, live Western program (broadcast from backlot studios in Philadelphia, of all places), but 'Hopalong Cassidy' was a filmed series, William Boyd having

BELOW: *A man, a land, and a dream. Walt Disney and a scale rendering of Disneyland, the construction of which precipitated his studio's entrance to television.*

acquired the rights to his own group of movie serials. A show that ought to have been done on film (because of the technical challenges to be overcome) was DuMont's 'The Plainclothesman,' with Ken Lynch. The viewer never saw the detective played by Lynch, only everything *he* saw: the direct gaze of people spoken to, doors being pushed open, a lighted match coming toward the screen to light his cigarette. Although this was produced live (and led to its full share of gaffes), a program like 'I Love Lucy' – basically produced on static stage sets – was filmed before audiences.

TOP: *Captain Video points the way . . . to some inevitable pokey, cheap-set destination, but also to the new television genre of sci-fi series.*

LEFT: *Richard Crane and Sally Mansfield were the stars of Rocky Jones, Space Ranger.*

Episodic drama fell into several categories. By its nature, dramatic series almost *had* to be pigeonholed. Live drama did anthologies, and the varied nature of presentations was one of its characteristics. Episodic drama aimed toward predictability. Westerns, crime shows, science fiction, medical dramas . . . these were the comfortable niches into which producers settled their programs.

'They Stand Accused' was a re-creation of court cases, the forerunner of such shows as 'Divorce Court,' 'Traffic Court' and 'The Peoples Court.' It ran on DuMont from 1948 to 1954, with the audience sitting as the jury. Another DuMont series was 'Rocky King, Inside Detective,' with Roscoe Karnes, and yet another DuMont entry – an icon of Golden Age nostalgia and a symbol of low-budget hokum – was 'Captain Video.' The science-fiction hero was played first by Richard Coogan and then by Al Hodge in a five-day-a-week pastiche of absurd plots and cheap props that attracted a wide audience, demonstrating that quality and popularity are not necessarily related in the American public's standards. Many starving actors who later became major stars – like Ernest Borgnine, Tony Randall and Jack Klugman – got their starts on 'Captain Video.'

Buck Rogers and Flash Gordon were sporadically resurrected from old B-movie and serials vaults, but television itself provided competition to the classics' tinny guns and glorified-pajama spacesuits. Cliff Robertson starred in 'Rod Brown of the Rocket

OPPOSITE: *Roy, Dale, and Trigger.*

ABOVE: *George 'Gabby' Hayes, consummate comic sidekick but also host of an early Western anthology series.*

BELOW: *Gene Autry, the original singing cowboy. Like Roy Rogers, Autry was a composer and legitimate recording star before entering movies and television. Autry made his mark yodeling in the Jimmie Rodgers fashion before donning a stetson, and penned such legendary songs as 'That Silver-Haired Daddy Of Mine' and a string of Christmas novelty songs.*

RIGHT: *Gene on Champion, back in the saddle again, out where a friend is a friend.*

Rangers' (Jack Weston played a sidekick, Wormsey); and Roy Seffens was both writer and star of the time-travel 'Captain Z-RO.' A favorite of children was 'Rocky Jones, Space Ranger' with Richard Crane, and a favorite of adults was his mini-skirted assistant Vena Ray, played by Sally Mansfield. Richard Webb played 'Captain Midnight,' until the conflict with the comic-book superhero of the same name caused the program to be renamed 'Jet Jackson, Flying Commando'; his side-kick was played by Sid Melton. And there was television's own version of 'Flash Gordon,' with Steve Holland in the title role.

Other atom-charged space operas of the primitive Golden Age included 'Commando Cody,' with Judd Holdren; 'Space Patrol,' with Ed Kemmer; 'Atom Squad,' with Bob Hastings (who later was Lt Carpenter of 'McHale's Navy'); and the famous 'Tom Corbett, Space Cadet,' starring Frankie Thomas.

Hoppy was not a lone cowboy on the small screen; many prominent Grade-B heroes rode into the sunrise of television. 'The Chuck Wagon' ran every day but Saturdays on CBS in the late afternoon, and in 1950 Gene Autry, his horse Champion, and sidekick Pat Buttram, hosted a syndicated half-hour and signed off at each happy ending with the song 'Back in the Saddle Again.' Roy Rogers ('King of the Cowboys') and Dale Evans ('Queen of the West') hosted their adventures beginning in 1951 and lasting 15 years. By the way, Trigger was the horse, Pat Brady was the sidekick, and 'Happy Trails to You' was the theme. Occasional guests on 'The Roy Rogers Show' were The Sons of the Pioneers, the cowboy singing group that Rogers had started in the 1930s when he was still Leonard Slye; at the time of the television show the Sons included Lloyd Nolan, Hugh Farr, Karl Farr and Lloyd Perryman.

Gabby Hayes, before he became television's resident second banana on horseback, had his own program, an anthology show of Western serials. He also punctuated the program with notes about Western lore and recollections of Hollywood service beside Roy, Gene, Hoppy and John Wayne.

'A fiery horse with the speed of light . . . a cloud of dust, and a hearty "Hi-Yo, Silver!" The Lone Ranger! With his faithful Indian companion Tonto, the daring and resourceful masked rider of the plains led the fight for law and order in the early West. Return with us now to the thrilling days of yesteryear! The Lone Ranger rides again!' These words – over the strains of Rossini's 'William Tell Overture' – marked one of the most familiar favorites of the Golden Age. Based on the successful books by Fran Striker, and the popular radio serial, 'The Lone Ranger' began his television crusade for justice in the old West in 1949 and only retired, except for re-runs, in 1961. John Hart, briefly, and then Clayton Moore, played John Reid, the Texas Ranger who swore vengeance for his brother's murder; Mohawk Indian Jay Silverheels played Tonto.

Feminism in the Old West came in the person of Annie Oakley, one of television's none-too-historical re-creations of Western legends. Gail Davis played Annie between 1953 and 1958; Brad Johnson played Sheriff Craig and Jimmy Hawkins played Tagg, Annie's brother. With an eye toward the future, perhaps, 'The Cisco Kid' began his exploits as a Latino Robin Hood in 1951 as the first television series filmed in color (color broadcasts were many years down the

trail); Duncan Rinaldo was the Kid, and Leo Carillo was the paunchy Pancho. 'Sky King' was a Western with a twist – a cowboy who flew a plane. Kirby Grant played former naval aviator King, and Penny King, his niece, was portrayed by Gloria Winters, who had been Jackie Gleason's daughter on 'The Life of Riley.'

'Wild Bill Hickok' was a syndicated, filmed Western (it was hard to do those chases on small sets live, even if the rocks were papier-maché, as in 'The Lone Ranger'). Guy Madison was in the title role and Andy Devine was Jingles ('Hey, Wild Bill . . . wait for me!'). 'The Range Rider' was Jock Mahoney, and his sidekick was Dick Jones as Dick West. 'Kit Carson' was Bill Williams, and *his* sidekick (every hero has one, kids) was Don Diamond as El Toro. 'Brave Eagle' made Indians the heroes, with Keith Larsen in the title role, Keena Nomleena as an Indian friend, Keena, and Bert Wheeler as half-breed Smokey Joe. 'Broken Arrow' was another series that depicted the Indian sympathetically; John Lupton played Tom Jeffords of the US Army, negotiating safe passage for Pony Express riders and fighting white men's prejudice; Michael Ansara played Cochise.

'Buffalo Bill Junior' was portrayed by Dick Jones, and 'Judge Roy Bean' saw gravelly voiced character actor Edgar Buchanan in the title role as a shop-keeper fed up with lawlessness and proclaiming himself 'the law west of the Pecos.' Douglas Kennedy played 'Steve Donovan, Western Marshal,' and '26 Men' starred Tris Coffin as the leader of the Arizona Rangers (limited by law to 26 in number) who represented the Law in the last days of the Old West. Just to the east were 'Tales of the Texas Rangers,' with Willard Parker as Jase Pearson starring in episodes illustrating the Ranger's battles with lawlessness between 1830 and the 1950s. More tales were told by Dale Robertson, narrator and star of 'Tales of Wells Fargo.'

Scott Forbes portrayed Jim Bowie, inventor of the Bowie knife and hero at the Alamo, in 'The Adventures of Jim Bowie.' And Rex Allen – the very last of the singing cowboys in movie serials – played Dr Bill Baxter, 'Frontier Doctor,' the man who dispensed justice and pills in the Old West. Allen remained a presence on television as a narrator for many Walt Disney documentaries and as a voice-over on countless commercials.

On the 'Disneyland' *Frontierland* series, a Western that ran for several episodes and frequent re-runs virtually chased the other guys out of town by sunset. 'Davy Crockett,' based – again, loosely – on an authentic Western hero's life, starred Fess Parker as the trail-blazer, lawmaker and Alamo defender, with Buddy Ebsen as sidekick George Russell. Segments depicted Crockett as an Indian fighter, a Tennessee legislator and US Senator, and at the Alamo, all in a Disney-style documentary effort to blend history and entertainment. History was secondary to the children of America, who went wild singing the theme song and wearing licensed replicas of Crockett's coonskin cap. 'Davy Crockett' was the last popular Western before television transformed the genre into a new category, the Adult Western, in the mid-1950s.

LEFT: *Annie Oakley (portrayed by Gail Davis), the Golden Age's cowboyette, replete with six-shooters and pig-tails.*

OPPOSITE TOP: *The Lone Ranger and Tonto (Clayton Moore, Jay Silverheels) striking a blow for racial parity as they subdue members of each other's caste.*

TOP LEFT: *Every cowboy hero had to have his colorful comic sidekick, and Jingles, played by Andy Devine, was among the most memorable, lending his girth, gravelly voice and accident-prone proclivities to the concerns of Wild Bill Hickok (played by Guy Madison).*

TOP RIGHT: *Kit Carson, typical of Golden Age cowboys who never seemed to sully their fancy duds.*

ABOVE: *A white sombrero and black shirt with fancy Mexican embroidery were trademarks of Duncan Rinaldo's Cisco Kid, which was already, at the time of its premiere in 1951, popular fare in books, magazines, radio and movies; it was to be a successful King Features comic strip as well, drawn by Argentine cartoonist José Luis Salinas.*

Mysteries and cop shows were staples of early Golden Age television. Again, many were on film because location-switches and wide pan shots were necessary. 'Martin Kane, Private Eye' was probably the first major success in this genre, although its antecedents in pulps, radio and movies were unashamedly clear. Running six years beginning in 1949, the dogged sleuth was portrayed by, in turn, William Gargan, Lloyd Nolan and Lee Tracy. In the last season, 'The New Adventures of Martin Kane' saw a switch in locale from the streets of New York to the capitals of Europe, with the P I played by Mark Stevens.

One of the most famous modern-day fictional detectives is Ellery Queen, who has been portrayed by a whole gallery of TV actors through the years. 'Ellery Queen' was a DuMont program between 1950 and 1955, with Richard Hart, Lee Bowman and Hugh Marlowe in the title role during its run. For two seasons on NBC in the late 1950s, George Nader and Lee Philips played the detective, and in the mid-1970s Jim Hutton would also portray him.

'Dragnet' made Joe Friday to television what Sherlock Holmes was to literature and The Shadow to radio. Jack Webb – creator, producer, writer, star – fashioned the police-procedural series into a television classic. Fans appreciated its unglamorous, realistic depiction of routine police work; detractors criticized the wooden acting. Actually, Webb sought a documentary mood and even used amateurs – occasionally the people involved in the actual cases upon which an episode was based – resulting in less-than-flashy performances. In a television-era update of Raymond Chandler's first-person narration, Sgt Friday would talk the viewers through the dates, times and places of the investigation, straight from the police blotter. 'The story you are about to see is true,' ran the opening. 'The names have been changed to protect the innocent.' The pervasive monosyllables and monotones would have been inappropriate in any medium but half-hour television: on the small screen it translated into intimate, compact slices of life. Friday's work on the Los Angeles Police Department ran from 1951 through 1959, neatly encompassing the Golden Age (the series was revived from 1967-70). Friday's sidekicks through the years were Barton Yarborough as Sgt Ben Romero; Barney Philips as Sgt Jacobs; Ben Alexander as Officer Frank Smith; and, in the '60s version, Harry Morgan as Detective Bill Gannon. 'Just the facts, Ma'am,' as Friday was wont to say impassively.

Other sleuths of the tube included Billy Redfield, star of 'Jimmy Hughes,

OPPOSITE: *Ever since Sherlock Holmes, the best detectives have smoked pipes, and Martin Kane was no exception. Silhouetted Lee Tracy was the third of four Kanes.*

ABOVE: *Jack Webb as the quintessential Golden Age cop Joe Friday of Dragnet, seen here with his 1960s sidekick Bill Gannon (Harry Morgan).*

'Rookie Cop'; Bruce Seton, as 'Fabian of Scotland Yard'; Jay Jostyn, reprising his radio role, and, later, David Brian as 'Mr District Attorney'; Rod Cameron, who starred in three crime shows of the Golden Age, 'City Detective,' 'State Trooper,' and 'Coronado 9'; and Kent Taylor as 'Boston Blackie,' another figure refashioned from short stories and radio.

'Man Against Crime' – in this case named Mike Barnett – had two television runs, played successively by Ralph Bellamy and Frank Lovejoy. Another hero with two lives on TV schedules was Mark Saber; Tom Conway starred in 'The Mark Saber Mystery Theater' in the early 1950s, and Donald Gray popped up as 'Saber of London' (one-armed Chief Inspector of Scotland Yard) in the late '50s. In syndication the latter version was titled 'Uncovered.' Boris Karloff portrayed the eye-patched 'Colonel March of Scotland Yard' in 1958.

Anthology police shows included 'Wanted,' introduced by Walter McGraw and 'The Man Behind the Badge,' narrated by Charles Bickford. Everett Sloane starred in 'Official Detective,' supposedly documenting actual police cases. Roland Winters and Stacy Harris played undercover agents on secret international missions on 'Doorway to Danger,' and Reed Hadley was the 'Pubic Defender' involving himself in crimes and mysteries. 'The Lawless Years' was a 1920s period piece starring James Gregory, who would later be another detective in the comedy series 'Barney Miller.' Victor Jory starred as Lt Howard Finucane in 'Manhunt' and Wendell Corey as Capt Ralph Baxter in 'Harbor Patrol.'

Herbert Philbrick, the courageous FBI man who played double-agent, documented his exploits – and Communist subversion – in a best-selling book, *I Led Three Lives*, and Richard Carlson portrayed Philbrick in the popular television series of the same name. Broderick Crawford played Chief Dan Matthews of the pavements in the memorable 'Highway Patrol'; 'ten-four' was his signature sign-off over his car-radio. Caesar Romero, movie idol, played diplomatic courier Steve McQuinn in 'Passport to Danger.' Lee Marvin played tough-guy Lt Frank Ballinger of 'M Squad' (Chicago Police Department) that sometimes skirted legal niceties, in the syndicated series of that name. 'Sea Hunt' – as producers stretched for new premises and locales – featured Lloyd Bridges as underwater troubleshooter Mike Nelson.

One of the era's tenuous premises was in 'I Cover Times Square,' with Harold Huber as Johnny Warren, crusading columnist, whose beat was the out-of-town newspaper stand in New York. 'Big Town' was built on a similar theme (as well as a radio hit series in which Edward G Robinson briefly starred), with Steve Wilson, the crime reporter, and Lorelei Kilbourne, the society reporter, joining forces to fight corruption. Among the many actors who revolved in these roles between 1950 and 1956 were Patrick McVey and Mark

Stevens as Wilson, and Margaret Hayes and Mary K Wells as Lorelei. Another newspaperman who played sleuth was David Chase, portrayed by Edmund Lowe, in 'Front Page Detective'; Frank Jenks played his contact in the homicide department. 'Crime Photographer' featured another newsman, Casey, played by Richard Carlyle and then Darren McGavin. In the age when 'Life With Father' and 'The Trouble with Father' were hits on the air, 'Crime with Father' – about a homicide detective and his amateur-sleuth daughter – tried it as a series, starring Rusty Lane and Peggy Lobbin. Perhaps the strangest (or, on the other hand, the most predictable) twist of all was 'Cowboy G-Men,' combining two sure-fire genres, with Russell Hayden and Jackie Coogan. The sure fire went out, however, as the program lasted only through the 1952 season.

Among other crime/cop/mystery shows of the early Golden Age were: 'Dangerous Assignment' with Brian Donleavy; 'Mr and Mrs North' with Joseph Allen and Mary Lou Taylor (after

the first season the famous sleuths were played by Richard Denning and Barbara Britton); 'Mr Broadway' with Craig Stevens and Horace McMahon; 'Waterfront' with Preston Foster; 'The Lone Wolf' with Louis Hayward; 'The Crusader' with Brian Keith; 'Wire Service' with George Brent, Dane Clark and Mercedes McCambridge; and 'Meet McGraw,' with Frank Lovejoy in the title role as 'a professional busybody who wanders from state to state minding other people's business.'

In the mid-1950s – just about the time of the Adult Westerns, a category discussed below – a new breed of mystery and crime shows made their appearance. Some were more intellectual, to be sure, but others were formulized and action-oriented (in contrast to analytical). The fact probably is that television, having been packed to overflowing with such programs, felt the need to vary the hackneyed procedural shows and the far-fetched premises. So in the latter 1950s, producers offered flashier procedural shows (usually featuring eccentric supporting players) and even more far-fetched premises.

'Perry Mason' made its debut in 1957 after years as a popular lawyer-hero in books by Erle Stanley Gardner and on radio. Raymond Burr played the title character, who not only never lost a case, but usually uncovered the *real* killer (or thief or embezzler) in the last moments of the episode, confounding

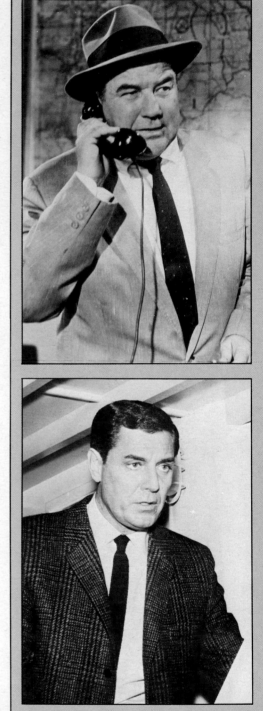

LEFT: *Warner Bros' line leader with their new spate of episodic/action dramas in mid-Golden Age was 77 Sunset Strip, starring (left to right) Efrem Zimbalist Jr, Edd (Kookie) Byrnes, and Roger Smith.*

TOP: *Broderick Crawford, son of Depression-movie hoofer Helen Broderick, was the Golden Age's toughest bulldog cop in Highway Patrol.*

ABOVE: *Movie producer Blake Edwards (Pink Panther, '10,' SOB) made his directional debut on TV's Peter Gunn, starring Craig Stevens.*

OPPOSITE TOP: *The sleuth with the law degree – Erle Stanley Gardner's Perry Mason (played by Raymond Burr, here with Barbara Hale) won every case.*

OPPOSITE BOTTOM: *Lee Marvin established his tough-guy image as the star of M Squad.*

the browbeating and evidently dense district attorney Ham Burger, played by William Talman. Authentic courtroom procedures seemed irrelevant to the writers . . . and also to the viewers, who swallowed the 'hook' of watching clues unfold through the hour and seeing Mason successfully pick the wildest of hunches. Through nine seasons 'Perry Mason' was one of the most popular shows on television. Also in the cast were Barbara Hale as Della Street; William Hopper (son of gossip columnist Hedda Hopper and originally considered for the lead role) as investigator Paul Drake; and Raymond Collins as Lt Tragg.

'Richard Diamond, Private Eye' was played by David Janssen in a stylish detective series with hip music by Pete Rugulo. One of the recurring devices in this series was that Diamond's professional life was completely run by his assistant 'Sam,' a secretary who was never seen on screen but for her shapely legs. The legs and voice were played at first by Mary Tyler Moore; Barbara Bain appeared on screen in later episodes as Diamond's girl friend. Another program with a suave leading man, sexy girl-friend and jazzy score was 'Peter Gunn,' produced by Blake Edwards of later 'Pink Panther' fame. Craig Stevens played the Private Eye, with Lola Albright as his girl, Edie Hart; Herschel Bernardi played Lt Jacoby on the program, which featured hip music by Henry Mancini and a title theme that became a hit record.

Another hit record, and show, was a program that actually represented a new formula for episodic drama. '77 Sunset Strip' revolved around a Hollywood detective agency, its PIs, its parking-lot attendant, loads of glamorous girls, humorous lines, fights and chases. In the cast were Efrem Zimbalist Jr as Stuart Bailey, with Roger Smith (as Jeff Spencer) and Richard Long (as Rex Randolph) as his partners. Jacqueline Beer played receptionist Suzanne Fabray, and character actor Louis Quinn played race-track sharpie Roscoe, their legman. The surprise hit of the series — the catalyst, and a magnet for teenaged-girl viewers — was Edd Byrnes, who played Kookie, the parking attendant (later a junior detective in the agency). In the first episode he played a heavy, but Byrnes adopted routines — like constantly combing his hair in the duck-tailed style of the day — that caught the attention of America's young. Besides the series' theme music, a song, 'Kookie, Kookie, Lend Me Your Comb,' became a national hit.

But the show was influential in a wider sense. It was the major hit series of a new formula — a team of private

eyes, a colorful sidekick, an inevitable collection of bizarre suspects – and a new format, one hour in length, an emphasis on action over plot, characters over clues. (These factors, as well as hip talk and music, reveal '77 Sunset Strip' as a precursor to 'Miami Vice.') Many of these shows were produced by Warner Bros, which reversed its lowly financial position in Hollywood by churning out these new formula episodic dramas – almost all of them virtually interchangeable except for locale and theme music.

Representative of such shows in the later years of the Golden Age were: 'Hawaiian Eye' with Robert Conrad, Anthony Eisley, Grant Williams and Connie Stevens; 'Adventures in Paradise' with Gardner McKay, Guy Stockwell, James Holden and Lani Kai; 'SurfSide 6' with Troy Donahue, Van Williams, Lee Patterson, and Diane McBain; 'Bourbon Street Beat' with Andrew Duggan, Richard Long, Van Williams and Arlene Howell; 'The Alaskans' with Roger Moore (later The Saint and James Bond), Jeff York and Dorothy Provine; 'The Roaring Twenties' with Rex Reason, Donald May, Gary Vinson and Dorothy Provine; 'Sugarfoot' with Will Hutchins; and 'Bronco' with Ty Hardin.

Warner Bros' biggest success was with a Western . . . or rather a Western spoof. James Garner played the lead in 'Maverick' as a fast-talking, gambling womanizer not especially fast on the draw, and more cowardly than any other cowboy on the screen. It typecast Garner, as he happily reprised the character type (in series like 'The Rockford Files' and many movies) and delighted legions of fans through the years. The setting was the old West and the hero usually got the worst of the chases and fights. The formula was so refreshing – and scripts and acting so sterling – that the Warners' structure was immediately in place: Jack Kelly played Bret's brother Bart, and eventually Roger Moore was added to play the boys' British cousin, Beau. Diane Brewster played Samantha Crawford, a female con artist counterpart of the Mavericks.

Warners had entered the television field in the same back-door manner as Walt Disney, sensing the opportunity to use the tube to place one-hour weekly commercials for their theatrical films. They were surprised at the public response and were prescient enough to seize the chance to become a major producer in the new medium. "Warner Brothers Presents" hit the air in 1955, and was ostensibly a group of four rotating titles. 'Conflict' was a simple drama anthology featuring Warners stars. Then two series – billed as sure-fire hits – were modeled on legendary Warners theatrical releases: 'Casablanca' (with Charles McGraw as Rick Jason) and 'King's Row' (with Jack Kelly, Robert Horton and Victor Jory). And, oh, yes: a third series to round out a full television

OPPOSITE, TOP: *Warners transferred their formula of episodic/action shows to the 50th state in 1959 with Hawaiian Eye, starring (left to right) Robert Conrad, Anthony Eisley, Connie Stevens.*

TOP: *James Garner as Maverick, a landmark type.*

ABOVE: *Clint Walker as Cheyenne.*

LEFT: *Maverick was a refreshing twist on the Warners formula . . . and on all types of television Westerns: the heroes connived and sweet-talked as much as they punched and shot. Taking their shots are Jack Kelly, Roger Moore and James Garner.*

dramatic fare: 'Cheyenne,' with young Warners contract player Clint Walker. This Western became the surprise hit, and the two 'sure things' as well as the anthology simply died on the vine. The *raison d'etre* for the entire enterprise disappeared too — the 10-minute segment hosted by Gig Young called 'Behind the Scenes,' hyping Warners movies. The public loved that Western show about the tall loner trained in the ways of the Indian, and 'Cheyenne' soon became an independent entry on prime-time schedules. (Walker also became the first of television's contract hold-outs. He received the salary of a bit player — below that of his guest stars — and was required to work in three movies a year, on the same conditions, without residuals. When he walked off the set, Warners discovered that the series could not survive without him . . . and *they* might not have survived without 'Cheyenne' at the start.)

One of Golden Age television's most memorable episodic dramas was a spin-off from from a two-part dramatic presentation on 'The Desilu Theatre' — 'The Untouchables.' Based on the real-life squad of incorruptible (hence their nickname) law-enforcement agents during Prohibition, the series was done documentary-style, with moderately realistic portrayals of confrontations during the Gangster Era. Robert Stack played Eliot Ness, who 30 years earlier had supplanted G-Man Melvin Purvis as

the government's most effective enforcement agent, but who only on television received widespread public notice. Neville Brand played Al Capone, in occasional appearances, and some of Hollywood's heaviest heavy guys, including William Bendix, Nehemiah Persoff and Lloyd Nolan, portrayed other gangsters. During 'The Untouchables' run, Italian-American groups protested the number of Italian surnames among the gallery of gangsters. The historically accurate series began in 1959 and ran through 1963 before syndication; it was narrated in the staccato, radio-style delivery of Walter Winchell, lending a documentary air and period flavor.

'Pete Kelly's Blues' was even more evocative than the superbly appointed 'Untouchables.' Set in Kansas City in the 1920s, the series starred William Reynolds as Kelly, a cornetist in a jazz combo, through whose eyes the viewer saw the flashier and seamier sides of speakeasies and Prohibition. The program featured many dark scenes and lonely cornet riffs as mood-setters.

Other episodic dramas of the period included: 'The Invisible Man,' with Lisa Daniely and Deborah Walting playing invisible man Peter Brady's sister and niece (the actor portraying Brady was never identified); 'Staccato' with John Cassavetes; 'Tightrope' with Mike Connors; 'Charlie Chan' with J Carrol Naish reprising his movie role, and James Hong as Number One Son; 'Whirleybirds' with Kenneth Tobey; 'Assignment: Foreign Legion' with Merle Oberon; 'Markham' with Ray Milland; 'Man with a Camera' with Charles Bronson; 'The Troubleshooters' with Keenan Wynn and Bob Mathias: 'Philip Marlowe' with Philip Carey; and 'Four Just Men,' about a group of World War II veterans who join forces to combat evils around the world, starring Dan Dailey, Jack Hawkins, Vittorio DeSica and Richard Conte.

OPPOSITE: The Untouchables – so called because they were incorruptible during the Tarnished Twenties – evoked genuine period flavor in the Desilu series.

LEFT: Robert Stack as Eliot Ness, real-life G-Man.

'The Naked City' was a superb cop show about the unglamorous side of urban police life. 'There are eight million stories in the Naked City,' ran the intro, and not all those stories were boring. Based on the screenplay by Mark Hellinger, legendary Broadway columnist, the television update starred John McIntire and James Franciscus; a later version starred Paul Burke and Horace McMahon. 'The Thin Man' was a stylish update of the Dashiell Hammett material, starring Peter Lawford and Phyllis Kirk as Nick and Nora Charles. Asta was, as always, their dog, and also in the cast were Nita Talbot, Jack Albertson and Blanche Sweet. 'The Third Man' bore no resemblance to the Graham Greene story or the Orson Welles movie. But memorable performances by Michael Rennie as Harry Lime and Jonathan Harris as assistant Bradford Webster made the syndicated series a favorite. The '50s' answer – in terms of popularity and stylisms – to Hammett and Chandler was Mickey Spillane, and Darren McGavin brought the Mick's hero, 'Mike Hammer,' to television in 1958-59.

ABOVE: Tommy Rettig, the first of Lassie's several owners, and one of several lassies and laddies who portrayed the canine lead.

LEFT: Guy Williams, star of Disney's Zorro.

OPPOSITE TOP: Noel Neill (Lois Lane) and George Reeves as Clark Kent, evidently exercising Superman's powers of X-Ray vision.

OPPOSITE BOTTOM: In a production shot (TV cameras were inside the 'room') we see what Superman flew into as he exited through windows.

Although it may not have always seemed so, not all of television's new episodic dramas were Westerns or crime/cop mysteries. Among other series of the Golden Age were: 'Pentagon Confidential' with Addison Richards; 'Navy Log' with a revolving cast; 'West Point' with Donald May; 'Terry and the Pirates,' based on the Milton Caniff comic strip and starring John Baer, 'Steve Canyon,' based on Caniff's later strip, starring Dean Fredericks; 'Riverboat' with Darren McGavin and Burt Reynolds; and 'Northwest Passage' with Keith Larsen and Buddy Ebsen. 'Robin Hood,' a British import, starred Richard Greene, and two Walt Disney-produced series were also successful costume pieces: 'Long John Silver,' starring veteran character actor Robert Newton, and 'Zorro,' starring Guy Williams. Alan Hale Jr, son of a classic motion-picture heavy and himself destined (or doomed) to play Skipper on 'Gilligan's Island,' portrayed Casey Jones, the railroad engineer, in the series of the same name.

Somehow a television Tarzan only hit the scene in the 1960s, but a former movie Tarzan, Johnny Weismuller, returned to the jungle as star of 'Jungle Jim,' based on the Alex Raymond comic strip. Another comic-based jungle epic was 'Sheena, Queen of the Jungle,' based on Jerry Iger's comic books and starring the statuesque Irish McCalla. Jon Hall worked the other side of the veldt as 'Ramar' – White Witch Doctor.

'Lassie' has been one of the most durable properties on television since the intrepid collie started wagging her tales in 1954; through the years there have been seven formats for the series, including one wherein there were no human regulars (the dog drifted from situation to situation, solving every crisis along the way) and an animated cartoon. During the Golden Age there were two casts: Tommy Rettig as Lassie's young owner, and Jan Clayton, George Cleveland and Donald Keller as supporting players; and (beginning in 1957) young Jon Provost as the dog's owner, with Cloris Leachman (later June Lockhart) as his mother, and Hugh Riley, George Chandler and Andy Clyde in supporting roles.

'Superman' was surely one of the icons of Golden Age television. The clunky special effects were overcome by the sheer audacity of the loud music, brassy narration and earnest performances. Christopher Reeves was the Man of Steel and, among his intimate friends who never discovered that he was also Clark Kent, 'mild-mannered reporter,' were Phyllis Coates, and later Noel Neill, as Lois Lane; Jack Larson as reporter Jimmy Olsen; John Hamilton as

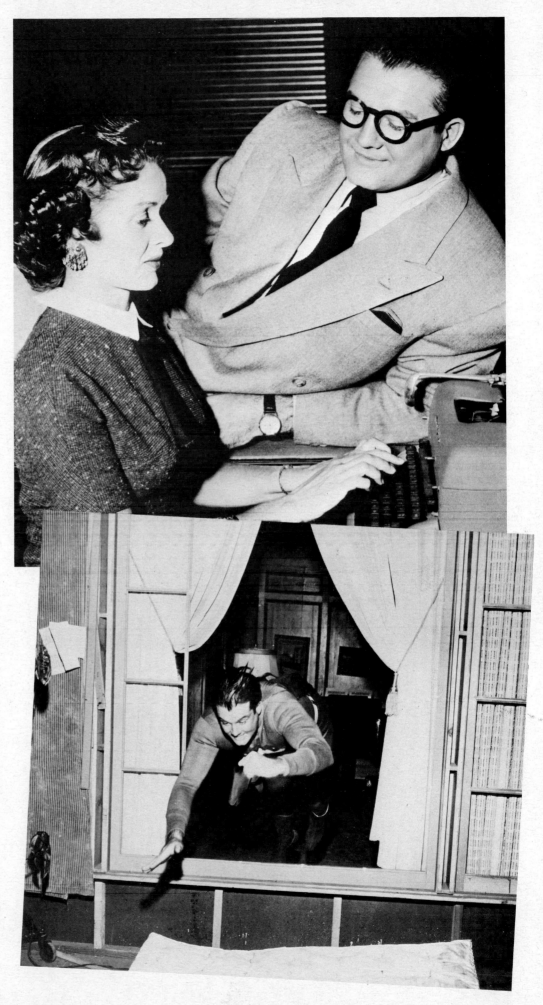

Editor Perry White ('Don't call me Chief!') and Robert Shayne as Police Inspector Henderson.

'The Adventures of Rin Tin Tin' fulfilled the dreams of every boy and his dog who watched the series. Inspired by the classic movie, the television series revolved around a young boy, Rusty, who was made a corporal at a cavalry base in Indian country so that he could stay with his soldier friends . . . and because his dog saved the life of Sgt Biff O'Hara. The boy was played by pre-teen Lee Aaker (the cavalrymen picked him up as the only human survivor of an Indian raid) and Joe Sawyer was O'Hara; James L Brown played Lt Rip Masters. Other animal series aimed at children included 'National Velvet,' based on the Elizabeth Taylor movie, with Lori Martin; 'My Friend Flicka,' based on the popular book by Mary O'Hara, with Johnny Washbrook and Anita Louise (the horse Flicka's name meant 'Little Girl' in Swedish); and 'Fury,' another series about a boy and his horse, with Bobby Diamond and Peter Graves (the brother of James Arness of 'Gunsmoke').

'Captain Gallant of the Foreign Legion' starred Buster Crabbe, a hero of countless Saturday-morning movie serials, and his son Cuffy. 'Circus Boy' listed the young, blond star's name as Mickey Braddock, but a decade later he was known as Mickey Dolenz, one of the Monkees. 'Sergeant Preston of the Yukon' was a refreshing change of scenery (even if the snow was fake); its star was Richard Simmons in full Mountie regalia.

In 'Medic,' Richard Boone became a certified television star (as Dr Konrad Styner), and the medium received its first sophisticated hospital drama series. The program, which ran from 1954 to 1956, was produced by live-drama veteran Worthington Miner. 'Mandrake the Magician' was yet another program based on a comic strip, this one by Lee Falk; Coe Norton played Mandrake and Woody Strode his servant, Lothar. The same year (1954) another strip inspired a syndicated series, 'The Joe Palooka Story'; the boxing comedy starred Joe Kirkwood Jr as the heavyweight champ, Luis Van Rooten (and later Sid Tomack) as manager Knobby Walsh, Cathy Downs as girl friend Ann Howe and Slapsie Maxie Rosenbloom as trainer Humphrey Pennyworth. (Palooka's creator, Ham Fisher, was also co-host of a children's program on DuMont – with Johnny Olsen – called 'Kids and Company.')

LEFT: *Ward Bond as wagonmaster Seth Adams in Wagon Train, the closest television has come to an epic saga. Bond, who died during the series' run, had a different role in the 1950 movie (Wagonmaster) on which the show was based.*

'The Millionaire' provided not only absorbing stories for its many loyal viewers, but a few vicarious dreams as well. Marvin Miller played Michael Anthony, the assistant to multi-billionaire John Beresford Tipton, a recluse (with voice provided by animation veteran Paul Frees) whose hobby it was to present folks selected at random with a million tax-free dollars. Mr Anthony would dutifully present the checks to the surprised people, and viewers would see if the windfalls saved or ruined their lives. Some episodes were stark tragedies, and some were comedies (with laugh tracks), but all of the anthology episodes were entertaining; 'The Millionaire' was one of the Golden Age's cleverest premises.

The biggest innovation in episodic drama, however – and the category series that sealed the doom of live drama – was the Adult Western. As suggested above, the creative adjustment may have been precipitated by little more than a logjam of themes and premises. In any event, the Western – certainly one of America's most durable fictional forms – was, on television, heretofore child's fare, with the same fights, chases and resolutions between good guys and bad that children watched on Saturday mornings in theaters. Television Westerns had grown, but not grown up. In the mid-1950s, however, a new breed of horse-opera appeared; there was less violence, more talking, and gray areas of moral ground. The new cowboys didn't sing, and they even got dirty.

To be sure, many of the 'new' Westerns were just as shallow as their predecessors, but they were superficial in less hackneyed ways, and at the time that translated into video refreshment. But other adult Westerns were, in fact, quality programs, with thoughtful premises and fine performances. Before the trend had run its course, it not only brought a slightly more sophisticated wrinkle to dramatic programming, but it resulted in a virtual thematic stampede. The late 1950s were awash in Western series; in 1959 alone, the new television season offered 21 Westerns in prime-time!

'Gunsmoke' was the series that opened the virtual Land Rush in the field, although other series premiering the same week in 1955 were also dubbed Adult Westerns. 'Gunsmoke' was transferred from its radio ride (where William Conrad, later Cannon and Nero Wolfe on television, was its hero's voice) and starred James Arness as Sheriff Matt Dillon. John Wayne, by the way, who introduced the first episode, had first been offered the lead role; Arness, the second choice, would play Matt until 1975 in one of television's

longest runs. The program was set in Dodge City, Kansas, and featured not only the realistic interplay between sympathetic and interesting continuing characters, but the problems, passions, sorrows and dangers of those who rode through town. There was gunfighting aplenty (the opening credits rolled over a showdown on the main street, and in Britain the stories were titled 'Gun Law'), but there was talking, too, and some of it fairly intelligent. In one more departure, the program was slated in the 10 o'clock time period – aimed squarely at adults, not children.

Other cast members through the years included Amanda Blake as Miss Kitty of the Long Branch Saloon; Milburn Stone as Doc Adams; Dennis Weaver as the gimpy deputy, Chester; Ken Curtis as Festus; and Burt Reynolds as blacksmith Quint Asper.

'Cheyenne' had made its debut the same season as 'Gunsmoke,' and so did 'The Life and Legend of Wyatt Earp,' which was coincidentally also set in Dodge City. Hugh O'Brian played Earp with television's typical denial of historical accuracy (Earp, and many other models for television Western heroes, was a real character, but no one said Adult Westerns made them documentary), and he was the first to cross the fashion line. The character dressed like a dandy – with string tie and patterned silk vest – but was soon to be outdone. When Gene Barry starred in 'Bat Masterson' with even more elegant attire, viewers cared less about differences from historical accuracy than differences from Hoppy, Roy and

ABOVE: James Arness in Gunsmoke.

BELOW: Hugh O'Brian portrayed Wyatt Earp.

OPPOSITE: Clint Eastwood of Rawhide.

Gene's head-'em-off-at-the-pass horse operas.

'Wagon Train' assumed the proportions of a saga. Its plot device was perfect – a wagon train of the 1880s,

traveling from the Midwest to California, was populated by an endless stream of people who brought their hopes and dreams, fears and pasts, and would join or leave the wagon train as plots dictated. There would also be changes of locale and the requisite encounters with Indians. Through its life span from 1957-65, it ran in one-hour as well as 90-minute versions. Ward Bond – one of the movies' quintessential cowboys – was the original trailmaster, Seth Adams. After his death in 1961, grizzled John McIntire took the reins as Chris Hale. Robert Horton, and later Robert Fuller, served as the inevitable young handsome scouts; and the cast included Frank McGrath, Terry Wilson, Denny Miller and Barbara Stanwyck.

Another classic show that employed the transcontinental motif had a similar run (1958-66): 'Rawhide' concerned the life and adventures of members of an 1860s cattle drive between San Antonio, Texas, and Sedalia, Kansas. Eric Fleming played Gil Favor, the trail boss, and country-music comedian Sheb Wooley played Pete Nolan, trail scout. But the centerpiece of the series was the character of Rowdy Yates, the ramrod, portrayed by Clint Eastwood. The actor parlayed his role into a career of movie Westerns beginning with the 'spaghetti Westerns' of Italian director Sergio Leone, which probably came closer to Western reality than any television shows or American movies.

'Have Gun – Will Travel' was probably the most adult-of the Adult Westerns. Offbeat, moody, and very successful was this series about the surly, mysterious hired gun known only as Paladin. Richard Boone starred as the gnarled gunfighter dressed in black who offered his services around the West to the helpless and oppressed. He had two trademarks: the paladin chessboard symbol on his holster, and a business card (business card? cowboys in the 1870s?) reading 'Have Gun – Will Travel. Wire Paladin, San Francisco.' Among the small regular cast were his servants, Hey Boy and Hey Girl, played by Kam Tong and Lisa Lu. Boone would later star in 'Hec Ramsey' in the 1970s, one of television's most intelligent Westerns.

'Restless Gun' starred John Payne, movie veteran, and 'Trackdown' featured Robert Culp as Ranger Hoby Gilman, years before his bigger successes as star of 'I Spy' and 'The Greatest American Hero.' Pat Conway was the star of 'Tombstone Territory' as Sheriff Clay Hollister in Tombstone, Arizona, 'the town too tough to die.' Wade Preston played Kit Colt, an arms salesman peddling the 'civilizer' in the untamed West in 'Colt .45.' In one of the many Westerns that still run (a lot of them on CBN Cable), with black-and-white film actually adding to their flavor, John Russell and Peter Brown starred in 'The Lawman,' as Marshal Dan Troop and Deputy Johnny McKay of Laramie, Wyoming. And Jeff Richards played the lead in 'Jefferson Drum,' about a newspaper editor and widower fighting corruption in the gold-mining town of Jubilee in the 1850s.

Steve McQueen made his first major mark on Hollywood by starring as Josh Randall, bounty hunter, in 'Wanted – Dead or Alive,' where his trademark was a sawed-off .30-40 calibre carbine rifle he called 'Mare's Laig.' In the series (spun off from 'Trackdown') he would have to contend with both bad guys he captured and less-scrupulous bounty hunters. Rory Calhoun made a bigger name for himself in television than in the movies, whence he came, as star of 'The Texan.' Television offered another career haven to Chuck Connors, one-time pitcher for the Dodgers. He played Lucas McCain, a rancher and widower attempting to raise his son in New Mexico. McCain's special weapon was a quick-action .44-40 Winchester carbine, which he twirled like a pistol, and which helped the town's marshal rid the neighborhood of bad guys.

Other Westerns included 'Yancey Derringer' with Jock Mahoney as the New Orleans dandy who concealed a tiny pistol in his hat; X Brands played

TOP LEFT: *Among a group of Westerns that hit TV screens like settlers at the Oklahoma Land Rush was* The Texan *starring Rory Calhoun (with Chill Wills).*

TOP: *Steve McQueen charmed farmgirls and viewers alike as Josh Randall in* Wanted: Dead or Alive.

ABOVE: *In* Colt .45, *Wade Preston played a gun salesman.*

OPPOSITE TOP: *America's generational saga with spurs was the Golden Age classic* Bonanza.

OPPOSITE, BOTTOM LEFT: *While* Wagon Train *and* Rawhide *trekked the plains,* Laramie *was set at a rest stop.*

OPPOSITE, BOTTOM RIGHT: *Henry Fonda in* The Deputy.

ABOVE: *He had a gun, he travelled, and he shot, but Richard Boone as Paladin was TV's cerebral hero.*

three sons, all borne by different wives who had each left Ben widowed. So it was the four single men, in this patriarchal saga, against the world – intruders, territorial lawbreakers, local politicians, vagabond swindlers and, occasionally, romantic interests of each of the Cartwrights. It was a magical formula for an episodic drama: Would they ever marry? Who would show up next? Could the sons sublimate their sibling rivalries to defend the Ponderosa?

Canadian Lorne Greene starred as father Ben Cartwright, and his sons were played by Pernell Roberts (introspective Adam), Dan Blocker (good-natured, bearish Hoss), and Michael Landon (impulsive Little Joe); among the four, every character trait in Central Casting's book was manifested, so every viewer had something to take away.

Something else was firmly taken away, too: the last commercial reasons for the production of live drama. With the runaway success of the major episodic dramas at the end of the 1950s, the live drama – so recently a proud symbol of television at its best – seemed as remote, and was as welcome, as dinosaurs in the networks' corporate boardrooms. 'Bonanza' could provide a large, loyal viewership across a wide spectrum; 'Hawaiian Eye' offered sumptuous locations; 'Maverick' presented clever writing and characterizations; 'Perry Mason' supplied suspense and mystery; and '77 Sunset Strip' – and many other series – were filled with action.

The genre of the live drama, as well as the anthology program which it spawned, seemed not only primitive but precarious to executives anxious to keep as many viewers' eyes as possible glued to their networks. The word was no longer 'show,' it was 'series.'

As an evolution, it was bound to happen, and many of the episodic dramas were fine productions indeed – probably even more integral to the new medium of television as it asserted its own language and structure, borrowing less from stage and cinematic forms. And it can be argued strongly that the Golden Age of the episodic drama occurred in the closing years of the '50s – television's larger Golden Age. Except for a few exceptions ('I Spy,' 'Secret Agent,' 'The Avengers,' 'The Defenders,' 'The Fugitive,' and 'Upstairs, Downstairs' come to mind), television would be bereft of consistent quality in its episodic series until the 1980s. Once again the early years provided the most memorable bursts of innovation and entertainment.

'Tune in next week,' America was told. And America did.

his Indian companion, Pahoo-Ka-Ta-Wah. 'Cimarron City' starred George Montgomery; 'The Rebel' featured Nick Adams as Johnny Yuma, and a hit record as its theme. 'The Tall Man' totally distorted the legend of Pat Garrett and Billy the Kid, but proved a serviceable vehicle for viewers who didn't care and its stars, Barry Sullivan and Clu Gulager. 'The Man From Blackhawk' was Robert Rockwell, playing Sam Logan, an insurance investigator in the Old West.

While many unknown actors became big stars via the television Western, Henry Fonda starred in 'The Deputy' as Marshal Simon Fry, and flopped after two seasons. Another movie veteran, Joel McCrea, starred with his son Jody in 'Wichita Town.' In 'Laramie,' Robert Fuller and John Smith played two friends who ran a ranch-and-station stop on the Great Overland Stageline; Hoagy Carmichael and Spring Byington were also featured. Earl Holliman

played Sundance – a name not inspired by the Sundance Kid, but by the ring of reflecting mirrors on Holliman's hatband – in 'Hotel de Paree'; and in 'Johnny Ringo,' Don Durant played a reformed gunslinger.

Other Westerns included 'Buckskin,' with Sallie Brophy and Tommy Nolan; 'Shotgun Slade' with Scott Brady; 'Tate' with David McLean; 'The Overland Trail' with William Bendix and Doug McClure; 'The Rough Riders' with Kent Taylor; 'The Californians' with Adam Kennedy and Richard Coogan; and 'Black Saddle' with Peter Breck and Russell Johnson (who would later play the Professor on sitcom 'Gilligan's Island').

A Western with as much soap opera, comedy and family melodrama as shoot-'em-up scenes was 'Bonanza,' which made its appearance in 1959. The premise had Ben Cartwright settling the enormous Ponderosa Ranch near the Comstock Lode in Nevada, raising his

SCANNING THE DIAL
Kids, Games, Soaps and More

ANUT GALLERY

'Quiz Kids' was a radio transition, a game show testing the knowledge of the schoolage set – ages six to 16 – producing some notable scholars (it was cancelled before the age of the quiz-show fixes). Joe Kelly was the first adult host, and in its last season (it ran 1949-56) the host was television's resident intellect, Clifton Fadiman. 'The Big Top' was one of several circus shows aimed at children. At first on CBS's prime-time schedule, it moved (1950-57) to Saturday afternoons. 'The Big Top''s base was Camden, New Jersey, where many circuses boarded off-season. The Ringmaster-host was CBS radio standby Jack Sterling, and the clown was Ed McMahon, who later performed a similar function on 'The Tonight Show.'

The fondly remembered 'Andy's Gang' began as 'Smilin' Ed's Gang' in 1950, sponsored by the Buster Brown Shoe Company. Ed McConnell, a white-haired bear of an uncle, played host, read from storybooks, sang and played the piano, talked to a collection of puppet animals and introduced movie segments like 'Gunga, the East Indian Boy.' When Ed died in 1954, Andy

Devine – a veteran second banana in movies and a ubiquitous character actor – took over. His sets were always strangely dark, and the gravelly voiced Andy spent much of his time on air with Froggy the Gremlin, whom he would exhort to 'plunk your magic twanger, Froggy!' amid puffs of smoke. Among the human sidemen were Alan Reed (later the voice of Fred Flintstone) and Billy Gilbert (consummate sneezer and classic veteran of Laurel and Hardy shorts). The puppets' voices included that of June Foray, certainly the most talented of female voices in cartoons and children's television.

'Andy's Gang's' appeal to young audiences and immediate success provoked a proliferation of puppets, among which was 'Rootie Kazootie,' another memorable creation. This baseball fan-boy wore his hat to the side and vented his enthusiasm through a kazoo. His five-day-a-week adventures (and parallel Saturday shows) always saw Rootie outwitting his enemy, Poison Zoomack. Todd Russell was the host of this series, which enjoyed a comic-book incarnation as well.

OPPOSITE: *Andy Devine switched from character roles in Westerns (such as Wild Bill Hickok) to hosting the Golden Age children's classic Andy's Gang.*

BELOW: *Todd Russell was the host of Rootie Kazootie during its 1950-54 run. The puppets were Rootie, the ultimate Little Leaguer, Gala Poochie, and sweetheart Polka Dottie; Deetle Dootle was the mute Keystone-type cop who helped the cast fight Poison Zoomack.*

'Mr Wizard' was a Golden Age classic that set about to be decidedly educational, and was a much-awarded pioneer in its field. Don Herbert was Mr Wizard, who demonstrated interesting scientific principles with simple, household-item materials to one or two youngsters in his 'lab.' The program generated more than 5000 Mr Wizard Science Clubs across the United States and enjoyed a run until 1965; it was resurrected in the early 1970s, and in the '80s on cable. Also educational, but aimed at a younger audience, was the beloved 'Ding Dong School' with Miss Frances (educator Frances Horwich). The matronly schoolmistress read and sang, taught basic reading, writing, and 'rithmetic, and conducted playtimes in coloring and finger-painting, an activity that must have delighted mothers at home. 'Ding Dong School,' besides being an enjoyable morning half-hour for children, was one of television's answers to early protests about violence and superficiality in children's fare. 'Ray Forrest's Children's Theater' was a potpourri of entertainment and information on Saturday mornings in New York; sponsored by Ronzoni, periodic filmed visits to the macaroni factory were part of its educational fare (Jack

Paar later parodied this by offering film-ed 'documentaries' of harvesting time in the Italian pasta groves, with spaghetti dutifully cut from trees and laid in the sun to dry). 'Children's Corner' was originally a replacement for Paul Winchell and Jerry Mahoney's children's programs; the hostess was Josie Carey, with her puppets and stories. The producer was Fred Rogers, who also served as puppeteer, voice-man and costumed guests. Rogers later took the show and concept – more than mere entertainment, social values were imparted to the unsuspecting young audience – to a local Pittsburgh station and thence to Public Broadcasting, where it was transformed into 'Mr Rogers' Neighborhood.'

'Winky Dink and You' is one of the most memorable children's programs because of the gimmick of the 'magic screen' for which parents were invited to send money at the behest of their viewer children. Winky Dink was a cartoon character who would invariably fall into scrapes, and the clues or solutions appeared on the screen, at which time kids were asked to affix the plastic green sheet to the television screen (it often stayed, by static) and trace lines with a crayon. Partially revealed letters and sentences were also thus recorded. Jack Barry was host to this potential desecration of the console's 'window,' and he parlayed this genuine bit of jollity to status as host and producer of many game shows, including 'Twenty One' (which was heavily involved in the fixing scandals), 'Tic Tac Dough' and 'Joker's Wild.'

Soupy Sales hit children's television like a pie in the face in 1955, after several years of local programs in Cincinnati and Detroit. Almost a spoof of kids' shows, 'The Soupy Sales Show' featured puppets – although they were cynical, sarcastic animals whose humor was pointed to older sensibilities – and homilies; Soupy's advice, however, was laced with schticks. When admonishing young viewers to drink their milk, the sound effect would resemble that of a toilet flushing. Black Fang was a dark, grumpy puppet, and White Tooth was a sweet white dog – both seen only by their heads – actually the ill-concealed hand of sideman Clyde Adler. Reba, another character, was seen only inside a pot-bellied stove, and Pookie was a

OPPOSITE TOP: *'Gee, Mr Wizard!' Don Herbert's household experiments fascinated all youngsters.*

OPPOSITE BOTTOM: *Miss Frances of Ding Dong School.*

ABOVE: Soupy Sales, *favorite of children and hip adults as well.*

LEFT: *Jack Barry with Winky Dink.*

wise-cracking lion. When Soupy got off a punch-line – or in fact, when any other event would trigger it – a pie would appear from nowhere and splatter itself on his face. Soupy Sales's humor was of the in-joke variety, a mixture of corny vaudeville and veiled double-entendre; the stagehands were always howling off-screen. Eventually, as the show bounced around networks and syndication, celebrities vied for the chance to guest-star and be hit by a pie.

The role model for 'Mr Rogers,' and the trailblazer in a sensitive, educational, non-patronizing form of children's pro-gram that later included 'Sesame Street' and 'The Electric Company,' was an un-likely gray-haired gentleman in a coat with enormous pockets – Captain Kan-garoo. His daily dose of stories, songs, sketches, lessons, puppets and cartoons began in 1955. A fixture on the eclectic set was Mr Greenjeans (played by Lumpy Brannum), an inventive farmer; Cosmo Allegretti played incidental characters and was chief puppeteer. One of the memorable running seg-ments of the delightful and comfortable 'Kangaroo' hour was the Terrytoon spot, where Tom Terrific and Mighty Man-fred the Wonder Dog made their ani-mated presences known. Bob Keeshan, who played Captain Kangaroo, learned the final lesson that Miss Frances herself didn't – that children can feel more relaxed, more receptive to learning ex-periences, when the television setting and host don't resemble a classroom environment.

Nineteen fifty-five was a landmark year for children's television: 'The Mickey Mouse Club' also premiered. It was a show that typified the Disney approach to everything – each show was an extravaganza, with song-and-dance numbers, cartoons, serial adventures and homilies. There were adult hosts – Jimmie Dodd, guitar player, and Roy Williams, a big bear of a man who was a Disney animator – but the real stars were the Mouseketeers, a group which every child watching wished he could have joined. Sporting a cap with Mickey-Mouse ears and turtleneck sweaters (a piece of apparel that added to the appeal of such budding Mouseketeers as An-nette Funicello), the kids were more than Peanut-Gallery members: they sang, danced and acted like real troupers. Airing five days a week, there was a thematic arrangement to 'The Mickey Mouse Club' that also lent an atmosphere of show-biz hoopla to the affair. On Mondays, there was the 'Fun with Music' segment; Tuesdays, 'Guest Star Day'; Wednesdays, 'Anything Can Happen'; Thursdays, 'Circus Day'; and Fridays, 'Talent Round-Up.' Running serials, all produced by Disney, in-cluded 'Spin and Marty'; 'Border Collie'; 'Corky and White Shadow'; and 'The Hardy Boys.' Jimmie may have been the nominal host, but it was Mickey's club, and each show featured an animated bit with Mickey talking to young viewers. The memorable series ran in 30- and 60-minute formats daily and on Saturdays, and enjoyed a long run (or re-run) in syndication after its expiration in 1959.

Art Clokely was producer and anima-tor of a memorable character in chil-dren's television, a virtual cult hero. That figure was a little bit of clay, manipulated and posed in stop-action animation: 'Gumby.' After starring in his own little five-minute adventures on 'Howdy Doody,' Gumby and his horse, Pokey, moved their pixilated adven-tures to a half-hour spot on Saturday mornings. Clokely was also creator of 'Davey and Goliath,' a long-running stop-animation children's series pro-duced by the United Lutheran Church.

'Ruff and Reddy' was also animation, but not quite of the traditional sort. Producers Bill Hanna and Joe Barbera had left MGM Studios when financial woes closed the cartoon department

WALT DISNEY'S
MICKEY MOUSE CLUB
MOUSEKETEERS
1956 - 1957

JIMMIE DODD

ROY WILLIAMS

SHARON BAIRD

LONNIE BURR

BOBBY BURGESS

EILEEN DIAMOND

MARGENE STOREY

KAREN PENDLETON

CUBBY O'BRIEN

DOREEN TRACEY

TOMMY COLE

ANNETTE FUNICELLO

DARLENE GILLESPIE

JAY JAY SOLARI

SHERRY ALLEN

DENNIS DAY

LARRY LARSEN

CHERYL HOLDRIDGE

CHARLEY LANEY

OPPOSITE: *Bob Keeshan, who began his television career as Clarabell on Howdy Doody, was the beloved Captain Kangaroo.*

ABOVE: *The entire cast of Mouseketeers.*

RIGHT: *Dance numbers were among the prominent points that attracted young male viewers to Mickey's Club.*

(they were responsible there for the award-winning 'Tom and Jerry' cartoons) and tentatively ventured into the television field. Costs of traditional animation – detailed backgrounds, separate cels for every portion of action, 24 frames a second – were prohibitive for the maw-like schedule of television, so Hanna-Barbera developed a system of limited animation. 'Ruff and Reddy' was short on sophisticated action, but long on droll humor and strong comic characterizations. Children and sponsors both loved the dog-and-cat pair, who received their own show on Saturday mornings. The success of 'Ruff and Reddy' was the springboard for Hanna-Barbera's phenomenal string of popular shows in the 1960s and beyond – animation series like 'The Flintstones,' 'The Jetsons,' 'Huckleberry Hound,' 'Deputy Dawg,' 'Yogi Bear,' and many more.

'You Bet Your Life' was an ideal showcase for Groucho Marx, whether his conversations were spontaneous or not. The veteran comedian was able to display his insults and ply his puns, as contestants chose their categories and answered questions of varying difficulty ('What color is an orange?' Groucho once posed as a consolation question). George Fenneman was the announcer and butt of jokes, and the program featured a toy duck that would descend with $100 in its mouth if the contestants uttered the 'secret woid.' 'Tell them Groucho sent you,' the host would suggest after each commercial pitch, although he never disclosed what a shopowner was obliged to do in response.

John Daly, a self-consciously erudite, eternally tuxedoed host, was master of Goodson-Todman's 'What's My Line?'. In fact, all of the panelists were routinely clad in tuxedos and evening gowns (for the men and women, respectively: this was still '50s television). The whole affair suggested an upper-crust parlor game. Panelists, whose challenge it was to guess the contestants' occupations and the mystery guests' identities, included Arlene Francis, Dorothy Kilgallen, Bennett Cerf, Fred Allen and Steve Allen through the years.

'To Tell the Truth' had a similar premise – panelists grilling a contestant, although in this vehicle two guests were supposed to prevaricate beside the third 'honest' guest. Bud Collyer served as host, and rotating panelists included Tom Poston, Peggy Cass, Orson Bean, Kitty Carlisle, Polly Bergen and Bill Cullen, himself a game-show host ('The Price is Right,' wherein studio-audience contestants were invited to guess the retail values of piles of merchandise). 'I've Got a Secret,' hosted by Garry Moore and peopled by Bill Cullen, Henry Morgan, Steve Allen, and Betsy Palmer, was a similar game show where celebrities plied the amiable Third Degree.

'You Asked For It,' hosted by Art Baker, purportedly tracked down, at great trouble and expense, bizarre requests from viewers to see unusual items around the world. More likely it arranged to film unusual items, people and events and then created requests to match, but the show nevertheless provided eight years of video voyeurism to a large audience.

At least two programs trafficked in the hard luck of their contestants. 'Strike It Rich,' hosted by Warren Hull, featured out-of-luck folks who pleaded with the home audience for donations that would alleviate their plight; the winner was the biggest loser, virtually based on the volume of tears that were jerked from the audience. A similar show – truly one of the most bizarre in tele-

vision history – was 'Queen for a Day,' hosted by Jack Bailey. On this program, different women competed with one another to tell the most pitiful tale of personal disasters and reverses. The tears flowed on 'Queen for a Day,' too, as the winner usually sat sobbing uncontrollably on her throne, with cape, crown, and scepter, probably as she realized that her gifts would be immaterial to her mother's cancer or her husband's alcoholism. This was television at its sappiest, but 'Queen for a Day' and similar programs had large and loyal daytime audiences.

Bert Parks was one of the hosts, and former Miss America Bess Myerson one of the 'hostesses' (models) on 'The Big Payoff,' a melange of games and songs where practically everybody but Parks himself wore, and gave away, elegant mink coats from a spiral staircase in the middle of the studio. Bowtied Bud Collyer popped up again on 'Feather Your Nest,' wherein contestants could win trinkets or bedroom suites for their homes. Jan Murray hosted 'Treasure Hunt' as well as 'Songs for Sale' and several other game shows of the '50s. Other familiar faces on early television served stints as game-show masters: Eddie Bracken ('Masquerade Party'); Herb Shriner ('Two for the Money'); Jack Paar ('Place the Face'); Clifton Fadiman ('This Is Show Business,' on which George S Kaufman was a panelist); and Fred Allen ('Judge for Yourself'). Another memorable game was 'Name That Tune,' in which contestants had to run across stage and pull a bell cord when they recognized a ditty; John Glenn, years before becoming an astronaut, was one contestant. On 'Jukebox Jury,' a panel of performers judged songs instead of merely recognizing them, and 'Talent Search' provided air time to aspiring stars. 'The Great Talent Hunt,' on the other hand, was emceed by the sardonic Henry Morgan, who seemed to enjoy showcasing pathetic amateurs. As premises grew thinner, 'Who's Whose?' challenged panelists to guess the mates of contestants, and 'Who Pays?' endeavored to have panelists guess the contestant's employers. This last piece of mental gymnastics was emceed by Mike Wallace, who hosted game shows and acted before settling on posing questions as a profession.

'See What You Know' was an early game show that featured Bennett Cerf, Tex McCrary and S J Perelman. 'Candid Camera' was a long-running program, adapted from radio's 'Candid Microphone,' that caught unsuspecting folks 'in the act of being themselves' when cornered by some outlandish happening contrived by host Allen Funt. 'Twenty Questions' was a simple tele-

TOP: Bill Cullen was host of the Golden Age guessing game, The Price is Right.

FAR LEFT: Jack Bailey was host of Queen for a Day, truly one of television's sappiest offenses. Contestants would vie for audience sympathy via the most pathetic of tragic tales.

LEFT: Warren Hull hosted Strike It Rich, another tear-jerking 'game' that trafficked in contestants' personal disasters.

ABOVE: What's My Line? was the Golden Age's weekly, urbane parlor game. John Charles Daly (standing) was the host. In this 1957 show, Ernie Kovacs was guest quizzer.

version of the parlor game, and 'It's News To Me' was basically a current-events quiz. 'Can You Top This?' was another crossover, from the classic joke-filled game radio program and its panelists Harry Hershfield, Senator Ed Ford, Peter Donald and Joe Laurie Jr.

One of the most familiar faces on Golden Age television was that of Johnny Carson. He was a constant presence in both variety and game formats, in daytime and in prime time, with regular programs and summer-replacement shows. He began with 'Carson's Cellar,' a local Los Angeles show of comedy and variety, and in 1954 was emcee of the game show 'Earn Your Vacation.' In 1958 he inherited the game show 'Do You Trust Your Wife?' from Edgar Bergen and Charlie McCarthy and retitled it 'Who Do You Trust?'; he and his announcer, Ed MacMahon, moved four years later to the late-night time slot and 'The Tonight Show,' which finally ended Carson's tour of the schedules.

If some game and quiz shows sounded dippy, many were earnestly intellectual, or at least literate. 'The Last Word' revolved around the charming inconsistencies in the English language 'as she is spoke' (Bergen Evens and John Mason Brown were among the philologists), and 'What in the World' thrust archaeological artifacts at experts and challenged them to discuss the items' origins. 'Dr I Q' transferred its rather modest brain-twisters from radio, and 'Brains and Brawn' was established on the premise of pitting eggheads against athletes, competing on the turfs of each. Senior citizens matched wits – they were hardly going to run across the stage for a bell-cord – in 'Life Begins at Eighty' (sponsored, appropriately, by Geritol), and matched talents in 'Battle of the Ages.'

In 'Make Me Laugh,' professional comedians tried to force contestants to crack a smile, and in 'Laugh Line,' a panel consisting of Mike Nichols and Elaine May, Orson Bean, and Dorothy Loudon had to provide funny captions to cartoons. Dick Van Dyke was the emcee. Similar game shows had relied on cartoons: 'Draw Me a Laugh' featured cartoonist Mel Casson in 1949, and 'Quick on the Draw' spotlighted cartoonist Bob Dunn's talents the following year. 'Keep Talking' was a clever show whose object was to have contestants finish the accounts begun by others without skipping a beat. Carl Reiner was the host, and regulars included Morey Amsterdam, Danny Dayton, Joey Bishop, Peggy Cass, Paul Winchell and Pat Carroll.

The proper placement of the fine line between quiz shows and game shows on television is open to question, but

ultimately the question is silly. 'Truth or Consequences' and 'Beat the Clock' were self-evident game shows, because contestants performed ridiculous stunts, and the atmosphere was one of a children's playground. Quiz shows were the more traditional question-and-answer formats (second-generation radio, where visual shenanigans had been perforce sublimated) and, usually, more intellectual. 'Name That Tune' would have been a pure guessing game except for the races across stage and so forth, and 'What's My Line?' or 'I've Got a Secret' were urbane question-and-answer affairs; their literate ad-libs and smatterings of wit elevated them above mere quizzes.

The distinctions were blurred definitively in the latter part of the Golden Age, when the big-money game shows were ushered in. Most of them were challenges to knowledge and quick thinking on contestants' parts, and the subjects were very often arcane, at least to the average viewer. But game shows they were . . . as much for the viewers as for the contestants. Ironically, it was when producers began operating on this fact – when the bigger teases were at the viewers', not the contestants' expense – that the genre self-destructed.

Louis G Cowan, who had worked on radio's 'Quiz Kids,' had a brainstorm in 1955. To add pizzazz to television quizzes, big-money winnings could be offered, he figured, as well as lavish prizes. 'The $64,000 Question' was hatched as a summer replacement in 1955. Hosted by Hal March, it became

ABOVE: *Mike Wallace congratulates a winner on his $100,000 Big Surprise.*

OPPOSITE: *Host Hal March and happy winners of* The $64,000 Question.

the first game show where viewers, when shouting answers at their television sets, could not only have the satisfaction of thinking they knew more than the folks chosen to play the games, but also receive the excitement (or frustration) of voyeuristically *being* on that stage. Imagine! Average Joes could win several times their annual salaries by merely answering questions. Television was performing a new function in American culture. The sitcoms – those set in middle America, with spacious homes and non-working wives (and even husbands) whose set-ups scarcely mirrored *real* Middle America – gave rise to an expectation gap among viewers. Similarly, the game shows of the latter 1950s engendered a host of false values for which America was fast becoming identified around the world – get-rich-quick windfalls, glitz over substance, and, ultimately, the primacy of success over honesty.

'The $64,000 Question' featured one contestant at a time being asked category stumpers with cash prizes starting at one dollar and doubling, within 'levels,' for each correct answer. The top prize at the highest level was $64,000, and winning contestants had the weeks between shows to decide whether to proceed to the top prize. The program instituted a television cliché of the day,

Seeking Heart'; 'First Love'; 'A Time to Live'; and 'Concerning Miss Marlowe.'
Other shows in the complete list of all Golden Age soap operas include 'Golden Windows'; 'The Greatest Gift'; 'Modern Romances'; 'Road of Life'; 'Way of the World'; 'A Date with Life'; 'Doctor Hudson's Secret Journal'; 'Hotel

BELOW: *The 1949 Thanksgiving Day Parade in New York marked the dawn of a new day. It was televised, and the Marshal was Mr Television, Milton Berle.*

Cosmopolitan'; 'Kitty Foyle'; 'Today is Ours'; 'From These Roots'; 'Young Doctor Malone'; 'For Better or Worse'; and 'The House on High Street.'

The television soap opera, which has spawned more fan magazines and more myopic TV addicts than any other genre, has also spawned careers of many actors and actresses who went on to presumably greater heights in television and movies, including Alan Alda, Warren Beatty, Ellen Burstyn, Dyan Cannon, Sandy Dennis, Robert De Niro, Peter Falk, Dustin Hoffman, Anne Jackson, Jack Lemmon, Bette Midler and Daniel J Travanti.

Television during the '50s also presented several offerings that became American institutions. The Academy Awards, Hollywood's self-congratulatory bash, first appeared on the screen in 1953 hosted by Bob Hope (a role he was to fill for nearly two decades), and two years later the television industry itself duplicated the annual rituals with its broadcast of Emmy awards. Bert Parks, game show host, assured himself of enduring fame by hosting the annual Miss America Pageant from Atlantic City; his brash, toothy rendition of the song 'Here she comes . . . Miss America' cumulatively overshadowed the indi-

vidual contestants and their feats of talent and declarations of devotion to world peace. The 'telethon' became a Golden Age coinage, a combination of 'television' and 'marathon' strictly defined as a weekend-long appeal for donations to a growing number of charities that employed the format. (Bob Hope and Bing Crosby hosted an early telethon to raise money for the 1952 Olympic team.) The Thanksgiving Day Macy Parade in New York City became an annual television event with its enormous, inflated balloons of cartoon characters. The Rose Bowl Parade was New Year's Day's television fixture.

ABOVE: *The television bishop, Fulton J Sheen.*

LEFT: *Oral Roberts was the first of many Pentecostal preachers to grace the tube.*

OPPOSITE, TOP; *The legendary Jon Gnagy provided many youngsters with their first art instruction.*

OPPOSITE, BELOW: *In a landmark special shown on two networks, the Ford 50th Anniversary featured Ethel Merman and Mary Martin.*

Sports were the earliest of television's standard programming. In the days preceding the Golden Age, the reasons were plain: Events were held anyway; most sports occurred in fixed settings, necessitating a minimum of camera shifting; and certain sports, like boxing, were well lit and required little technical refinement in video or audio levels. Therefore the 'Gillette Cavalcade of Sports' and 'Boxing from Jamaica Arena' were early series. Two sports as hyped-up as they were violent owed their success to Golden Age television exposure: wrestling and roller derby. The Cotton and Rose Bowls came to television in 1954, thereafter to be as inevitable as hangover remedies on New Year's Day. In 1953 the struggling ABC introduced its baseball 'Game of the Week' with former pitching great Dizzy

Dean providing the 'color' commentary as few others could do. And NBC became the regular broadcaster of World Series games.

Religious programming had its home during the Golden Age, and most of it was, predictably, confined to Sunday slots. Many programs were aired as public-service obligations. During the 1950s each day's programming (there were no all-night stations) concluded with 'Sermonettes,' leading television evangelist Jimmy Swaggart to wonder later whether Christianettes resulted from the milkwater homilies. Among the mainstream religious shows were 'Lamp Unto My Feet,' 'Look Up and Live,' 'Frontiers of Faith,' 'This Is the Life,' and 'Crossroads.' Independent preachers and smaller denominations bought their own time, however, or broke into prime-time, and presented 'The Old-Fashioned Revival Hour' and 'The Hour of Decision with Billy Graham.' Bishop Fulton J Sheen was placed by DuMont on Tuesday nights against Uncle Miltie and often drew respectable ratings; when the prelate was named Outstanding Television Personality of the Year, Berle bowed to 'Uncle Fultie,' as he called him: 'That's all right. We both work for Sky Chief.' Norman Vincent Peale's variety of pep-talk Christianity became a television fixture in the '50s and Pentecostalism was represented by filmed tent-meeting revivals and the healing services of Oral Roberts.

One of television's earliest stars was Jon Gnagy, who hosted a program called 'You Are an Artist.' Clad in flannel shirt and sporting a goatee – in the '50s, his appearance confirmed that he *was* an artist, if not a downright nut – he drew copious numbers of spheres, cones and perspective lines while hawking the mail-order art supplies of Art Brown & Bros., New York. Ray Heatherton was another familiar face as 'The Merry Mailman,' host to kiddies through rain, snow, sleet and hail. Robert Ripley hosted the video version of his classic 'Believe It or Not' newspaper feature, and the urbane Sherman Billingsley interviewed celebrities from his table at 'The Stork Club'; his female counterpart as society chat mistress was Faye Emerson, whose low necklines provoked debate during the early '50s and probably accounted for her healthy ratings, if not brisker sales of television consoles. And Jim McKay, later a respected sports announcer, was the host of an unusual program called 'The Verdict is Yours'; the studio audience would serve as jury while professional actors, briefed only slightly, would improvise roles in court-room proceedings.

The Golden Age was alive with one-shot specials and occasional appearances by certain stars. Danny Kaye, for instance, eschewed a regular series and hosted a few fine variety spectaculars. Among television's most memorable specials during the Golden Age were: 'Irving Berlin's Salute to America'; 'The Ford 50th Anniversary Show' (broadcast simultaneously on NBC and CBS, and featuring Mary Martin and Ethel Merman among dozens of stars); 'Cinderella' (a version written just for television by Rogers and Hammerstein, with Julie Andrews and Jon Cypher); 'Art Carney Meets Peter and the Wolf' (with lyrics by Ogden Nash); 'An Evening with Fred Astaire'; 'The Diamond Jubilee of Light' (which aired on all four networks); and 'Dancing Is a Man's Game' (with Gene Kelly).

By the end of the Golden Age the airwaves were alive with programming of all sorts. It had been a scant dozen years or so since fledgling networks and a few independent stations scattered across the landscape had strained to fill the evening hours alone with solid programming entries. The question that obviously posed itself – especially after the quiz-show scandals – was whether more meant better. By most yardsticks, it didn't seem so, but more Americans continued to watch more television, on more sets (and more sets per household), for longer hours. RCA and NBC experimented with color broadcasts as early as 1953, and many viewers awaited the widespread utilization of the new technology . . . but no one postponed his daily doses of the tube in the meantime.

BIG BUSINESS
The News according to Television

As critics and industry executives surveyed the future of television at the dawn of the Golden Age, there was much ahead of them that could not have been foreseen. On the other hand, the evolution of many things – technological, thematic, conceptual – would be only a matter of time. After all, not only science-fiction writers, but scientists and inventors had been talking about the future of television since the 1880s. One of the predictions that never quite came true (in the Golden Age or since) was that television would be a miraculous conduit of culture – 'art galleries in the home,' glowed General David Sarnoff of RCA in the 1930s, as he forecast television's future. In America this has not happened to any respectable extent, and only cable television in the 1980s has allowed a candle to pierce the darkness.

Another prediction, however, appeared to come true, soon after America became a television society: the expectation was that television would bring news to the masses, offering instant information and illumination. Television could enlighten the indifferent, and bypass problems like illiteracy and prejudice. Indeed, in the Golden Age, television offered such events as Queen Elizabeth's coronation, coverage of the atom-bomb test at Yucca Flats, and Soviet leader Khrushchev's visit to the United States, at the proverbial flick of the switch. At worst, this coverage satiated viewers' curiosity; at best it made them more informed citizens – and (it was hoped), by extension, wiser voters. The coverage of political conventions cemented television's role and exposed more widely the statements and personalities of politicians.

Apart from strict news coverage, a documentary series about recent history, but with implications for current policy, was the excellent 'Victory at Sea,' featuring taut scripting, superb footage and powerful, original, musical scores. 'You Are There' was also documentary, with a strong dose of entertainment and fiction. The past was recreated for viewers as actors portrayed famous figures at crucial junctures in history. It was a unique concept, and its presentation, with Walter Cronkite as host, foreshadowed the blurred line between news and entertainment that was to arise during the Golden Age and never to be resolved thereafter.

PREVIOUS SPREAD: *John F Kennedy, already being touted for the Democrat presidential nomination, prepares for a 1958 appearance on CBS's* Face the Nation, *the Sunday morning interview.*

RIGHT: *Events like the landing at Leyte were documented on* Victory at Sea.

Victory at Sea, with its exacting research, seemingly inexhaustible historical footage, and superb original music by Robert Russell Bennett, set a standard for television documentaries that was not always followed by producers with axes to grind.

One of television's first 'personalities' was a news reader, John Cameron Swayze. He was short, silky and nasal, often sporting a boutonniere as he hit the airwaves in 1946 with 'The Camel News Caravan.' Swayze preceded countless 'television newsmen' (as opposed to print journalists) who were not reporters but could look nice on screen while reading words.

Many of the finest radio reporters shifted to the greener pastures of black-and-white television, although others continued to work on radio. Among this group, some of whom had honed their skills on World War II fronts, were Edward R Murrow, Walter Cronkite, Richard C Hotellet and Lowell Thomas. Douglas Edwards became a model of unobtrusive news-reading that few, unfortunately, emulated. Other notable news personnel included John K M MacCaffery, Howard K Smith and Pauline Frederick. John Charles Daly, host of the 'What's My Line?' game, was not only ABC News's nightly anchorman, but also director of new operations for the network, indicating once again that news was more than news — it was part of a network's image, to be packaged for consumers (viewers), and, perhaps, sublimated to commercial ends.

LEFT: *John Cameron Swayze.*

ABOVE: *Douglas Edwards, professional voice of CBS News, inaugurates the first portable TV camera in 1956.*

BELOW: *Lawrence Spivak informed, was an impartial interviewer and moderator.*

'Meet the Press,' with Lawrence Spivak at the helm as producer and moderator, moved to NBC Television from radio, and provided weekly press conferences with newsmakers from around the world. Spivak's insight and probing questions were a model of what the medium could offer viewers in order to make their own decisions about issue. CBS followed with a similar format in 'Face the Nation,' in 1954. Swayze and Daly looked like dilettantes when NBC

teamed Chet Huntley and David Brinkley in 1956. The anchormen's styles contrasted — Huntley was conservative and straight-forward, Brinkley liberal and glib — but they were stars. 'The Huntley-Brinkley Report' made their personalities paramount, and the switching from their New York and Washington desks lent a genuine sense of style to the show. Their 'good nights' to each other even rivalled the sign-offs of Dave Garroway (an upraised palm, and 'Peace') or Dinah Shore (throwing a kiss to the audience) in TV's lexicon. Thus began the rush to make the anchor persons telegenic stars, often chosen more for appearance or engaging personality than for journalistic experience or reportorial instincts. Television news programs — boasting relatively low overheads, with static sets and a succession of film clips — became big business for the networks, and $3-million annual salaries were in the industry's future; they would be awarded to stars who could hold audiences, not necessarily to newsmen who scored scoops or plied beats. From John Cameron Swayze's carnation to the blow-dried hair of today, style was doomed to dominate substance in television news presentations, and the Golden Age hurried the process along. Walter Cronkite only took over the 'CBS Evening News' from Douglas Edwards in the 1960s (before he was unceremoniously dumped a few years later, albeit temporarily, in a ratings war), and it was not until 1959, when Robert Trout hosted the 'CBS Saturday News,' that television had its first half-hour news program; 5 or 15 minutes had been the standard length until then.

LEFT: *The full studio set for the 1958* Face the Nation *broadcast. The CBS show, NBC's* Meet the Press, *and ABC's* Issues and Answers *all served similar audiences in similar time slots on Sunday mornings, and competed for the same newsmaking guests.*

BELOW: *Chet Huntley and,* BOTTOM, *David Brinkley, the first real stars of the evening news round-ups. NBC cultivated their personalities and format (each news reader was in a different city, tossing items back and forth), making Chet and David household names.*

OPPOSITE TOP: *The Crime Hearings of 1952 were big news. Television was there – and supplanting motion pictures on their own turf.*

OPPOSITE BOTTOM: *The hearings of Sen Kefauver (at center of panel) electrified the nation via television.*

Congressional hearings were a boon to early television, if for no other reason than that they offered the economical attraction that wrestling matches did – static sets, minimal production procedures, low overhead. In 1952 television had high drama placed in its lap when the hearings into organized crime, conducted by Senator Estes Kefauver and his committee, were televised. The star was mobster Frank Costello, who demanded that his face not be shown on television – privacy, not secrecy, was his motive, for these were public hearings – and when the industry complied, viewers were treated to dramatic close-ups of the gangster's hands during his testimony. The hands were symbolic and eloquent counterpoint to the underworld leader's words as they fidgeted, sweated and shifted constantly.

Network white papers and news specials were broadcast sporadically during the Golden Age. New documentaries would reach their peak – in influence and in numbers of productions – during the volatile, politicized 1960s, but again there was evidence that journalistic integrity was of secondary importance to the television industry. The documentary 'Hunger in America,' for instance, faked the malnutrition death of a baby seen on screen, and 'The Selling of the Pentagon' actually cut and spliced interview tapes to create different answers than respondents had offered. By that time (the 1960s) it was evident that television 'News' organizations put not only entertainment but propaganda ahead of news judgment and journalistic ethics.

The point became clear that the little box in everyone's living room *might* be a liberating educational device . . . but it could also be a powerful tool of influence. Charges were made that stations were flashing split-second images on the screen, and viewers were subconsciously being influenced on behalf of commercial products. But the up-front commercials themselves – broadcast time and again, with flashy visuals, catchy tunes, beautiful models and simplistic slogans – were pervasive and influential enough. Either method might have warmed the cockles of Josef Goebbels's heart, for here was a medium where millions of people sat glued to a machine that belched forth messages of persuasion; the viewers then dutifully following the 'suggestions.' In 1950 Hazel Bishop, Inc., sold $50,000 worth of cosmetics; then the company started advertising on television, and in two years revenues had risen to $4.5 million. The tale, of course, was repeated across the tube all through the Golden Age, and ever since. In the early 1940s, a commercial for Bulova watches during a televised Brooklyn Dodger game cost nine dollars; by the end of the Golden Age, 60-second commercials were pushing the $100,000 mark. Advertisers obviously believed they were getting some return for their money as they bought air time insatiably. In the mid-era year of 1956, for example, Procter and Gamble spent $55 million on friendly television persuasion; General Motors spent almost $49 million.

Advertising on television also tells a larger numbers story. In 1949 the four

networks lost a combined $25 million on their operations; at the end of the Golden Age, in 1960, the combined profits of the three networks (DuMont having expired) was $244 million. More specifically, in 1949, revenues from sales of national and local advertising was $7.28 million dollars, but in 1960, $469 million. Sponsors made their influence felt in the studios as well as the boardrooms: The American Gas Company dictated that all references to gas be removed – from the death-camp extermination exchanges in 'Judgment at Nuremberg'! A reference to fording a stream was excised from a program sponsored by Chevrolet, Ford Motor Company's competition. And in shows sponsored by an ad agency handling filter-cigarette accounts, all bad guys had to be shown smoking non-filter cigarettes.

In a brief review of the Golden Age's most memorable, or ingrained, commercials, the slogans are often what trigger the recollections: 'LS/MFT' (Lucky Strike cigarettes); 'Ajax, the foaming cleanser'; 'Made by tobacco men, not medicine men' (Old Gold cigarettes); 'Why don't you pick me up and smoke me sometime?' (Dutch Masters cigars), 'How are ya fixed for blades?' (Gillette, which was the routine sponsor of World Series baseball); 'Winston tastes good, like a – clap, clap – cigarette should!'; 'Does she or doesn't she?' (Clairol Hair Color); 'Look, ma! No

willing, even anxious, to suspend disbelief where television is concerned; Edward R Murrow, in his easy chair, and, later, Walter Cronkite (who would intone 'And that's the way it is') were perceived as trustworthy figures. Especially in the decade following the Golden Age, network news departments acted as if presidential speeches were merely the opening halves of debates, and such coverage would be followed by news 'analysts' almost invariably hostile to the politician.

Murrow and Friendly's 'See It Now' was a series of essays and profiles from the CBS news ministry. The documentaries focused on issues or personalities, and if their bias was predictable, so was their brilliant production technique. Murrow and Friendly traveled the globe for the material and haunted the editing rooms for pathmark techniques of camera angles, dramatic editing and cohesion. The series profiled the case of Lieutenant Milo Radulovich, whose family was accused of Communist connections. Annie Lee Moss, a witness before the McCarthy committee, was featured. There were interviews with Doctor Jonas Salk, General Dwight D Eisenhower, and General George Marshall. On-the-road reports were delivered from Korea, South Africa and racially torn Southern cities. None of this was impartial – it was what a later generation would call 'advocacy journalism' in newspeak – but it was brilliant television, introducing techniques and standards that many were to follow.

Murrow, before he finally left television to serve as Director of the US Information Agency under Kennedy, was host of 'Person to Person,' in which he sat before a huge television screen, puffing on his trademark cigarette, seeming to exchange eye contact with celebrities he interviewed in their homes. The celebrities – such disparate headline-makers as Norman Rockwell,

TOP: *Edward R Murrow was a virtual icon at CBS News.*

ABOVE: *Murrow and his producer Fred W Friendly set the tone for current-events series and advocacy programs.*

OPPOSITE: *During the Golden Age Murrow hosted Person to Person; here Jerry Lewis parodies his host. Special effects were more important than truth, as in this publicity shot where the screen of Jerry Lewis was superimposed to create an illusion.*

aids on wounds, but television's major windfall was the boost given to cultural programming, and the resuscitation of the dream of an educational network. When the Golden Age closed, this was still a dream, but just over the horizon were Julia Child ('The French Chef') and Max Morath ('The Age of Ragtime'), two engaging hosts whose programs were the first "hits" of the fledgling Educational Network, proving that the cult of personality is not exclusive to commercial television.

The Golden Age drew to a close in 1960 with the final breath of live drama and the virtual end of anthology drama; henceforth, action and adventure shows would supplant more introspective offerings. Situation comedies had ceased their emphasis on name stars as necessary components; the premise became more important than the star, but, unfortunately, also more important than the writing. The variety shows continued, but with none of the patina that shone so warmly around Berle, Caesar and Kovacs. The evolutions of game shows and television news had also ended many of the characteristics – not the least of which was innocence – of the Golden Age.

One reason it is so easy to identify the 1948-60 period as the Golden Age is that much of television was fairly awful immediately thereafter. The 1960s and '70s saw television become trivial about 'relevance' and earnest about pure fluff. The trees are still too thick to observe the forest, but many aspects of 1980s television may occasion some optimism. Not the least is the explosion of cable television, bringing great diversity to the screen and choices for viewers of drama, comedy, movies, sports, culture and – dare we say best of all? – countless re-runs of Golden Age television.

In a real sense, however, this menu of old and new in every field ironically fulfills, in a high-tech manner, what Golden Age television represented to the viewers who first responded to its magical appeal – something for everyone, everywhere, somewhere on the dial.

The Golden Age does not need an aura of nostalgia, nor a viewer's selective memory, to retain its status in television history or even in the broader history of American culture. It was a period of interesting innovation and brilliant experimentation, of memorable personalities and fascinating formats. It no longer mattered whether masses of viewers were gazing into the screens or, symbolically, staring at their own reflections. Because of Golden Age programming, Americans were virtually mesmerized by television, and it became a willing, happy servitude.

Marilyn Monroe and Fidel Castro – acted as if they had looked up to find Ed in their living rooms, but, of course, they had been invaded by corps of crewmen, lighting technicians and cameramen several days in advance. (The technique has survived in 'Nightline' and other programs where correspondents still pretend to be talking to images of their subjects.) 'Person to Person' was well done, and remains as a valuable record of innovative television and of important personalities who have left the scene.

In 1957 there was a news event that American television could not cover. The Soviet Union launched its *Sputnik* satellite, and the shock-waves were felt very widely indeed throughout America. The countdown was accelerated in several areas besides America's own space race. A new emphasis was placed on education (and federal education budgets), and television was an indirect beneficiary. Since the beginning of commercial television, educational programming was a stated objective of its founding fathers. Early in the Golden Age, there were educational-programming experiments at local stations – too local (i.e., without network support) and too few to have made any impact on the profile of early television, however.

But after *Sputnik*, with many government grants for science programs, with the International Geophysical Year proclaimed to promote scientific enterprises, and with the advent of cultural programs in American diplomacy, educational television received its impetus. Local stations were established, and daytime programming in languages and laboratories caused millions of American schoolchildren to huddle around portable TV sets in their classrooms.

Such exercises had the effect of band-

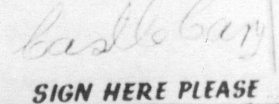

THE BRITISH SCENE

BY DAVID LAZELL

taken by Fred Streeter, one of the most popular broadcasters of his time. Prior to the outbreak of the war, Middleton had developed a small garden in the grounds of Alexandra Palace, from which programs were transmitted as he advised on the best methods of growing and nurturing various plants and flowers. With the war-time emphasis on growing food, the garden had been devoted to vegetables, still something of a preoccupation in 1946, when food shortages and rationing were still an everyday experience. Another early postwar program anticipated the booming interest in music hall and vaudeville (which shows no sign of diminishing all these years later).

'Late Joys,' a 1946 show, brought traditional music-hall entertainment, with actor Leonard Sachs as chairman. His polished style served the show well, and Mr Sachs went on to host one of the most successful of all television light entertainment shows, 'The Good Old Days.' Transmitted from The City Varieties Music Hall in the Yorkshire industrial city of Leeds, the show is unique in that it invites members of the audience to dress in Victorian and Edwardian costume, available freely on

loan at the theater. Thus viewers get a clear impression that they have indeed traveled to a music-hall theater as it was in the days of Marie Lloyd, Gus Elen and other 'greats.' Although the show is not being transmitted at this writing, its format is no doubt destined to run again, probably into the next century.

Another show of amazing continuing popularity is the panel game 'What's My Line?,' in which members try to guess unusual jobs mimed by visitors to the studio. Introduced in 1951, it has been revived since and was produced in 1986, with Eamon Andrews as quizmaster. As Andrews was the first quizmaster in 1951, he has earned a special niche in the history of light entertainment. The show brought to national discussion a somewhat irascible but greatly loved character, Gilbert Harding, a bluff, bespectacled man who sometimes seemed rather 'sharp' with the 'challengers.' All over Britain, viewers would ask friends and neighbors if they had seen Gilbert Harding last night! Yet he was an excellent member of quiz games on radio and a talented man.

As in prewar days, cabaret – in diverse guises – was included in the very limited BBC schedule, being easy

to produce and, on the whole, requiring little studio space, though some fast camera work was needed with acrobats and knife-throwers. The Saturday evening 'Cafe Continental' gave viewers the impression they were moving through smart swing-doors (saloon style) into a dining and cabaret area, to share the fun of the evening. Like other early programs, 'Cafe Continental' owed a great deal to the charm of its presenter, Helene Cordet. With the Sunday evening play (complete with interval, usually a country or similar scene, accompanied by quiet music), the Saturday evening show was the main entertainment of the week. The star-sequence format appeared in various guises, including 'Rooftop Rendezvous,' 'Starlight,' 'Music Hall' and 'Hulbert Follies,' presented by a well-known star of theater and movies, Jack Hulbert. Situation comedy of the kind that changed the face of television was almost unknown in the early 1950s.

Occasionally, though, the BBC presented a program that caught the public imagination. The drama production of '1984', with Peter Cushing as Winston Smith was certainly one, bringing the phrase 'Big Brother Is Watching You'

LEFT: *On the set of* Café Continental, *hostess Hélène Cordet and French actress Cécile Aubrey.*

OPPOSITE RIGHT: Café Continental's *orchestra leader Sydney Jerome.*

ABOVE: *Robert Brown and Ann Todd, stars of the BBC play* The Offshore Island.

into everyday conversation. Similarly, the BBC scored a great hit with its Saturday night sci-fi thriller serial, 'The Quatermass Experiment'. It posed the question: what kind of nasty influences might be waiting for astronauts in outer space? Given the limitations on television special effects, the program proved to have great impact on the population's viewing habits. 'Little Red Monkey,' another Saturday night thriller serial, had an unusual spin-off, when three radio stars recorded a song to the original electronic sound theme to the play. Sci-fi has had a somewhat mixed life in television, special effects

sometimes overtaking the importance of a good and understandable plot. One of the early successes of commercial television was the series 'One Step Beyond' which, in half hour teleplays, related often true-life stories of the virtually unbelievable, a mix of 'Believe It Or Not' and the stories of Ambrose Bierce or Edgar Allen Poe. It is perhaps strange that the format has not been revived.

Another gloomy view of the future was BBC TV's highly acclaimed 'Offshore Island,' which starred the film actress Ann Todd in a play written by Marganhita Laski. It was set in the near future when a largely uninhabitable Britain (tainted by radioactivity) possessed a small area of population, itself interpreted as a threat to prevailing international stability by competing world powers. Given recent events in the nuclear power industry, not to mention the abundant saber-rattling in the world, the play was almost prophetic.

In the early days of television-watching, there was no idea of using television as a background 'hum' as is often the case today. Domestic meal schedules sometimes revolved around the time that the BBC Play began. Neighbors calling for conversation, or a gift for the church bells fund, were steered to a vacant chair, given some light refreshment, and expected to stay quiet until the drama was over – or at the very least, until the halfway interval permitted some relaxation from the 12-inch tube. Perhaps that is one reason why people recall early 1950s programs with such clarity. They were the object of *study*; further, with such limited output, the BBC Sunday Play was the highlight of the week. Miss that, and you *might* catch the repeat on Thursday, but it could mean dislocation of other personal commitments. It is indeed this aura surrounding television, in terms of social behavior, that is specially mem-

Another legendary show from the mid-1950s was 'Dixon of Dock Green,' based on the everyday work of a policeman in the London area of 'Dock Green.' Written by Ted (later Lord) Willis, the show was a spin-off from a successful British movie, 'The Blue Lamp' – also about police work – and although it moved slowly by contemporary standards, it had the merit of a veteran actor, Jack Warner, in the title role. He was backed up by other excellent players, including Peter Byrne as Police Detective Sergeant Crawford, and while there were occasional car chases and other excitement, the episodes were as much about human relationships as catching crooks. The opening of the show, Dixon to camera, "Evening, All!" became a catch-phrase in Britain, and the show was used in adult education among much else to assess public attitudes to the police (then hardly a political issue as it is today in Britain). Jack Warner – no relation to the Hollywood studio chief – had already earned a sound reputation in music hall and on radio, as comic and singer of droll songs.

Police series developed along faster lines with 'Z Cars' (BBC) written by a series of contributors including Alan Plater. Set in 'Seaport' (sometimes

ABOVE RIGHT: *The canteen setting for the popular* Dixon of Dock Green.

OPPOSITE TOP: *A production still from BBC's* Z Cars.

BELOW: Jack Warner, star of Dixon of Dock Green.

identified with Liverpool) the series was a gritty, fast-moving show, showing that policemen were ordinary men, not saints. Stratford Johns as Chief Inspector Barlow did not have the soft style of Jack Warner's 'Dixon of Dock Green,' though a further police series, using the same character style as 'Z Cars,' was called 'Softly, Softly.' Some publications, mainly aimed at the children's market, were derived from the 'Z Cars' show, but even the latter programs explored human relationships in addition to showing action out on the street. Compared with the flood of police-and-crook shows, most of them imported from the US today, these early television shows would seem almost Shakespearean.

Once the Americans Dr Kildare (Richard Chamberlain) and Perry Mason (Raymond Burr) arrived on British television screens and, for that matter, appeared on the cover of the weekly BBC program guide, 'Radio Times,' the British were no slouches in making programs with medical or legal themes. Probably the best known of all shows was 'Dr Finlay's Casebook,' set in the village of Tannochbrae, Scotland, sometime between the two world wars, with veteran actor Andrew Cruikshank as the wise general practitioner (ie,

village doctor) while coping with the 'new ideas' of his assistant, played by Bill Simpson. Another popular broadcaster, Barbara Mullen, played the housekeeper. Andrew Cruikshank's Dr Cameron was almost, in relationship to Bill Simpson's Dr Finlay, that of Raymond Massey's Dr Gillespie to Richard Chamberlain's Dr Kildare – there the similarity ended. The Dr Finlay stories were based on A J Cronin's fictional but close-to-reality reflections on family medicine some 50 or 60 years ago. The BBC has immense expertise in period pieces (as it has proved time and time again, not least in a 1980s series based on the life of a North Country veterinary practitioner in the 1930s). Viewers might at times have picked up comments from the show, relating to their own long-running traumas, since Dr Finlay was nothing if not an embryonic psychologist. Well-known Scots comic and actor Andy Stewart made a popular record based on the characters in the series, 'Oh Doctor Finlay.' Pop records sometimes picked up television themes, and not only in musical scores. Al Read, a well-known radio comedian, produced an excellent monologue-song called 'Our Joe's Been Seeing Too Much Telly' (television), which was really something of a classic

comment on British attitudes to the medium.

Billy Cotton, a leading dance-band leader as long ago as the 1920s, moved into television in 1956. 'Radio Times' for 2 January 1959 has Billy Cotton on its cover, recalling his first broadcast as a

band-leader in 1928. His show had plenty of action, and in that sense, Billy Cotton understood the necessity of a video aspect to a band show. Earlier in the decade, another band leader, Victor Sylvester, was featured on the cover, in relation to one of the BBC's most suc-

ABOVE: *Billy Cotton, host of* The Tin Pan Alley Show *on BBC television.*

Goody Gumdrops and Other Puppet Prose

Puppets – on-string or glove variety – offered low-cost, relatively static programming, yet showed their possibilities in several early 1950s shows. Annette Mills (sister of the actor John – now Sir John – Mills) brought Muffin the Mule to the television audience, creating one of the all-time 'greats' of children's television. Muffin, a string puppet, danced on top of the grand piano, while Annette sang or talked to Muffin and his friends. The theme song, 'We Want Muffin the Mule,' was probably known by at least half the children in Britain, while another of Miss Mills' puppets, Prudence the Kitten, seems to have delighted youngsters almost as much as Muffin the Mule. However, Muffin did not have a 'voice,' but conducted conversation with Annette Mills by 'whispering' into her ear, or making suitable gestures, nodding its head, for example.

Marionettes, puppets and other in-

animate characters flourished in children's television. John Wright's Marionettes included 'Joey The Clown and his Catapulting Chair' as well as 'Achmudt the Sinister Sand Dancer,' while another early 1950s favorite – destined to have a long-running career – was Andy Pandy, presented by Maria Bird who wrote the script and music for this 'baby character.' The sign-off music, 'Time to Go Home,' became as well known as any chart success on the hit parade. Older children preferred characters like Hank the Cowboy, presented by his creator, Francis Coudrill. Hank had a voice (which belonged to Francis Coudrill) and looked like a real Westerner with his cowboy hat and drooping moustache. Francis Coudrill was (and is) a fine artist, and the story-line was always excellent. Like US characters – Charlie McCarthy for example – Hank had personality, and this was understandable, given that he appeared on the same show as Mr Turnip, probably the BBC's most famous puppet character.

The Saturday afternoon 'Whirligig' show was devised and produced by Michael Westmore, who – while aiming at a children's television audience – built up a family interest. Among performers in the show was musician Steve Race, who went on to host some of BBC's popular music quiz programs. Popular radio star Humphrey Lestocq joined the program as foil for the somewhat crusty character, Mr Turnip, a well-attired puppet who regarded this colleague as not at all bright. Humphrey Lestocq was addressed as 'HL' by the puppet, and the show abounded with such comments as 'Goody Goody Gumdrops' and 'Looky Lum!' Viewers recognized in the partnership something of the dumb one-bright one encounters in films and vaudeville, 'HL' being the dumb one.

OPPOSITE TOP: *From the serial* Lost Property *on* Whirligig *(1954),* Jack Stewart, John Gray *and* Ivan Craig.

OPPOSITE BOTTOM: *Also from* Whirligig, *Carol Lorimer is in boxer Freddie Mills' corner.*

ABOVE: *A superstar of British children's television was Muffin the Mule, here posing with Ann Hogarth and Jan Bussell.*

Picture Credits
The Bettmann Archive Inc: pages 10 (top), 11 (top), 12 (left), 13 (top), 14 (top), 15 (top), 18 (bottom three), 21 (bottom right), 26 (top), 27 (bottom), 28 (top), 31 (top), 32, 32-3 (top), 33, 34-5, 36, 39, 41 (bottom), 43 (all three), 44-5, 51 (right), 64-5, 70 (both), 71 (bottom), 80 (top), 81, 83, 116, 117 (both), 120 (bottom), 128-9, 129 (right), 130, 131, 133, 138 (both), 146, 154 (both), 155, 156-7.
BBC Hulton Picture Library: pages 129 (left), 158 (top).
Bison Picture Library: pages 4-5, 7, 8-9, 12 (right), 15 (bottom), 26 (bottom), 40 (bottom), 46, 46-7, 47 (bottom), 48 (bottom), 52, 55, 56, 57 (both), 58 (bottom), 59, 62, 86, 87 (both), 88-9, 90 (bottom), 91, 92, 93 (both), 95 (all three), 96 (both), 97 (all three), 99, 100 (top and bottom left), 101 (bottom), 102, 102-03, 103 (both), 104-05, 105, 106 (both), 107 (both), 110 (both), 112 (top right and bottom right), 113 (top and bottom left), 118, 121 (both), 123 (both), 124 (both), 125 (both), 126 (top), 129 (left), 139 (both), 151 (top), 178 (top), 179, 180.
Camera Press Ltd: page 170.
Department of Defense: page 144-5.
Granada Television: pages 171, 173.
Hallmark Hall of Fame: pages 76 (all three),

77 (top).
John F Kennedy Library: pages 140-1, 148 (top left).
Kraft, Inc: pages 72 (both), 73 (both).
Museum of Modern Art/Film Stills Archive: pages 2-3, 74.
National Archives: pages 142-3, 145 (right).
National Film Archive, London: pages 58 (top), 80 (bottom), 101 (top), 108-09, 172-3.
New York Public Library: page 149 (top).
Phototeque: pages 13 (center), 17, 18 (top), 19, 21 (center four), 40 (top), 47 (top), 53 (bottom), 61 (bottom), 86-7, 90 (top), 99 (bottom right), 114-15, 126 (bottom), 128, 134, 135, 148 (top right and bottom right), 150.
S & G Press Agency: pages 159, 160 (both), 161, 162 (both), 163 (both), 164, 164-5, 166 (both), 167 (both), 168 (both), 169, 174, 175 (both), 176, 177, 178 (bottom), 181, 182 (both), 183, 184 (both), 185, 186, 187.
Alex Siodmak: pages 14 (bottom), 31 (center), 66 (top), 68 (all three), 69 (bottom), 98.
Springer/Bettmann Film Archive: pages 22, 23 (all three), 25 (top), 37 (top), 51 (top left), 61 (top), 71 (top), 113 (bottom right).
TPS/Keystone: page 158 (bottom).
UPI/Bettmann Newsphotos: pages 66

(bottom), 132, 136-7, 147 (top), 149 (bottom), 151 (bottom), 152-3, 153.
US Navy: page 145 (left).
Wisconsin Center for Film and Theater Research: pages 10 (bottom), 11 (bottom), 12 (top), 13 (bottom), 14 (center), 16, 20, 24, 25 (bottom), 27 (top), 28 (bottom), 29 (both), 30 (both), 31 (bottom), 32-3 (bottom), 37 (bottom), 38 (both), 41 (top), 42 (both), 48 (top), 49 (both), 50, 51 (bottom left), 53 (top), 54, 60, 63 (all three), 67, 69 (top), 75, 77 (bottom), 78 (both), 79 (both), 82-3, 84, 85, 94, 111, 112 (top left and bottom left), 119, 120 (top), 122, 127, 147 (bottom).

Acknowledgments
The author and publisher would like to thank the following people who have helped in the preparation of this book: Robin L Sommer, who edited it; Jean Chiaramonte Martin, who did the picture research; Mike Rose, who designed it: Florence Norton, who prepared the index; Barbara Marschall and Lisa Weber, who assisted with the research and reviewed the manuscript (all opinions and any errors are the author's own however); and Hector Rodriguez, Barbara Ogourek and Pam Manser.